Immigrant Politics

Immigrant Politics

Race and Representation in Western Europe

Edited by
Terri E. Givens
Rahsaan Maxwell

LYNNE
RIENNER
PUBLISHERS

BOULDER
LONDON

 # 756166727

Published in the United States of America in 2012 by
Lynne Rienner Publishers, Inc.
1800 30th Street, Boulder, Colorado 80301
www.rienner.com

and in the United Kingdom by
Lynne Rienner Publishers, Inc.
3 Henrietta Street, Covent Garden, London WC2E 8LU

Library of Congress Cataloging-in-Publication Data
Immigrant politics : race and representation in Western Europe / edited by
Terri E. Givens, Rahsaan Maxwell.
    p. cm.
Includes bibliographical references and index.
ISBN 978-1-58826-830-3 (alk. paper)
  1. Immigrants—Political activity—Europe, Western.
2. Minorities—Political activity—Europe, Western. 3. Political
participation—Europe, Western. 4. Europe, Western—Emigration and
immigration—Political aspects. 5. Europe, Western—Race relations.
6. Europe—Politics and government—1945– I. Givens, Terri E., 1964–
II. Maxwell, Rahsaan.
  JV7590.I44 2012
  325.4—dc23
                                                    2011042447

British Cataloguing in Publication Data
A Cataloguing in Publication record for this book
is available from the British Library.

Printed and bound in the United States of America

     ∞ The paper used in this publication meets the requirements
        of the American National Standard for Permanence of
        Paper for Printed Library Materials Z39.48-1992.

     5 4 3 2 1

Contents

Foreword

We are witnessing a point in history where governments are being scrutinized for their ability to adequately serve their citizens. Much of the world is focusing on the political transitions taking place in the Middle East, but, like the authors of this book, I have called for a greater focus on the West. Many countries across North America and Europe are failing to live up to the democratic ideals of representation in government and access to full political participation for all citizens.

Governing institutions in North America and Europe tend to be unrepresentative of their populaces. In the United States, Barack Obama's election as president was a beautiful and symbolic victory, yet once he became president, no African American senators remained, and none appear to be on the horizon. In contrast, one would find an overrepresentation of minorities when visiting the service employees in the basement of Capitol Hill.

The authors of this book detail similar scenarios of underrepresentation and exclusion in Europe. These issues are not new, but they have a renewed sense of urgency as openly racist and xenophobic political platforms become increasingly common in Europe. Recent mass deportations of Roma from France, Italy, and other countries prompted Roma-inclusion efforts in the European Union. Additionally, the UN designation of 2011 as the International Year for People of African Descent has increased the focus on whether persons of African descent in Europe enjoy full political rights.

In April 2009, I worked in cooperation with current and former European Parliament members Joe Frans, Harlem Desir, Claude Moraes, and Glyn Ford to hold the "Black European Summit: Transatlantic Dialogue on Political Inclusion" at the European Parliament in Brussels, Belgium. The summit allowed a small group of legislators, minority leaders, and experts from more than ten countries in the Organization for Security and Cooperation in Europe (OSCE) region to exchange information on barriers to political participation and the roles of minority policymakers in representing minority interests, promoting equal rights, and combating discrimination. Following the event, participants adopted the Brussels Declaration on minority political participation and released a report.

The findings from our summit were similar to those in this book. First, the majority of our political and legal systems do not accurately reflect the racial and ethnic diversity of our societies. Second, minorities have not been sufficiently included in the development and implementation of government policies, including antidiscrimination initiatives. Third, there is not enough political will from governments, political parties, and other actors to include minorities in governance. Fourth, limited political knowledge among minority communities often makes it difficult to garner the necessary support to effectively address these issues.

The solutions we identified were also similar to those discussed in this book: advertising employment opportunities in minority communities; requiring the active recruitment and interviewing of minorities for positions; providing minority youth fellowships and internships; financing degrees for minorities in relevant fields such as law, international relations, political science, and economics; and facilitating involvement in public-private policy initiatives, such as the development of energy and trade policy.

Since 2009, we have continued to meet annually under the banner of the Transatlantic Minority Political Leadership Conference. In 2011, we called for the United States and European Union to adopt a cooperative strategy similar to the "U.S.-Brazil Joint Action Plan to Eliminate Racial and Ethnic Discrimination and Promote Equality" (2008) and the "U.S.-Colombia Action Plan on Racial and Ethnic Equality" (2010). We view a focus on minority political participation as a key component of any strategy. The United States and European Union have cooperated on issues of national importance from security to energy. Issues of diversity and inclusion are equally important for the long-term stability of our democracies and should be included on any strategic agenda.

This book provides the often missing historical background and data on minority political participation in Europe needed to bridge the racial divide on both sides of the Atlantic. How our nations choose to move forward will determine whether the ultimate strategy for the West will be inclusion or revolution.

—Alcee L. Hastings
Member of US Congress
Ranking Member,
Commission on Security and Cooperation in Europe

1

Ethnic Minorities and Political Participation in Europe

Terri E. Givens and Rahsaan Maxwell

In March 2011, at a conference in Brussels, ethnic minority elected officials from across Europe discussed their experiences in politics. As ethnic minorities, most were nonwhite and all were either immigrants or descendants of immigrants. They had spent most of their lives in European countries with few (if any) nonwhite elected officials as role models. The fact that there were now enough nonwhite politicians to hold a conference was a positive sign that barriers for representation were beginning to fall. Yet, many expressed frustration at the slow pace of progress and the lack of access to high-level political power for nonwhite ethnic minorities in contemporary Europe.

Nonwhite immigrant-origin communities are at the center of many political debates in Europe. In particular, many native Europeans are concerned that nonwhite immigrants and their descendants are failing to integrate. One of the most contentious examples is the debate over how to accommodate Muslim religious practices to a largely secular and historically Christian Europe. At times, this has led to legislation that limits the ways in which Muslims can practice their religion. In 2009, a Swiss referendum banned the construction of new minarets atop mosques, and several countries have either passed or debated restrictions on wearing headscarves, veils, and burqas (Moore 2010). Another point of concern is whether nonwhite immigrants and their descendants

suffer intractable discrimination. This has led some European governments to debate whether official forms of "affirmative action" should be
adopted or discouraged (Calvès 2008). Other political actors claim that
the problem lies with nonwhite ethnic minorities who have failed to sufficiently adopt European norms. This has prompted some governments
to restrict access to citizenship and more actively promote assimilation
(Joppke 2007a, 2007b).

All of these concerns generate intense policy debates. The fear that
ethnic minority immigrants are ruining European society has provided
fertile ground for xenophobic far-right political parties to insert themselves into the mainstream agenda (Givens 2005). In some countries,
these far-right parties have claimed up to 30 percent of the vote and
become part of the national government. However, on the other side of
the debate, there is relatively little ethnic minority representation, particularly in national parliaments. This raises questions about whether
the interests of ethnic minority immigrant-origin communities are being
adequately represented in contemporary European politics.

In this book we examine political participation among nonwhite
immigrant-origin ethnic minorities in contemporary Western Europe.
Drawing on media discourses, public opinion data, and elite interviews,
we analyze how European publics feel about nonwhite politicians, how
political parties are reaching out to nonwhite communities, and how
nonwhite communities feel about their political influence. Country-
specific chapters focus on Britain, France, Germany, and the Netherlands, the four countries with the largest nonwhite ethnic minority
communities in Western Europe. Underlying the analysis of Western
European developments is an implicit comparison with the United
States. In 2008, the United States elected its first black president,
Barack Obama, who promised to be a political "game changer." In
Western Europe, many nonwhites are hoping for similar opportunities.
In the chapters that follow, we reflect on the possibilities and the prob-
lems that nonwhites face in Western Europe and offer insight on what
countries on both sides of the Atlantic can learn from each other.

Immigration and the Development
of Minority Communities in Europe

One of the biggest challenges for nonwhite political participation in
Europe is the fact that most nonwhite communities in Europe are the re-

sult of post–World War II immigration. Most of these immigrants arrived without citizenship and could not vote in European countries. Moreover, in the early years of migration, European governments were not very aggressive about incorporating these immigrants into the mainstream political system. In part, this was because most nonwhite immigrants who arrived in Europe during the 1950s, 1960s, and 1970s were temporary workers. They were not expected to stay, so most governments did not plan for their integration. Yet by the 1980s and 1990s it became clear that these were permanent communities, and since then West European governments and societies have become more focused on promoting their full inclusion (Castles and Miller 2009).

It is important to note that European societies have dealt with the difficult issues of immigration, integration, and diversity for centuries. Yet prior to World War II, those migration flows were primarily within Europe. European migrants usually faced intense discrimination after arrival but over time and across generations were able to blend in with their fellow Christian Europeans. The new nonwhite immigrant communities in Europe challenge this trajectory because they are unable to physically blend in, even across several generations. Racial diversity is now a social and political issue in Europe in ways that are fundamentally different from the past.

Despite this increasing importance of racial diversity, however, issues of racism and discrimination have only recently gained the attention of policymakers in many European countries. Even throughout the centuries of colonialism, slavery, immigration, and ethnic conflict, European policymakers have consistently avoided addressing the issues of racism and discrimination. Britain is the one exception, where policymakers began developing race relations policies in the 1950s and 1960s. But from the more general legal architecture of the European Union (EU), it would appear that until recently most Europeans felt that race was not an important issue. For example, it was not until the 1999 Treaty of Amsterdam that the European Council empowered the European Commission to "take appropriate action to combat discrimination" based upon "racial or ethnic origin." Soon after, in 2000, the EU quickly developed an antidiscrimination policy, known as the Racial Equality Directive (RED), which has been transposed into national law in EU member states (see Chapter 7).

One main reason why European countries have been so reluctant to address the issue of race is the legacy of the Holocaust. During World War II, the concept of race was used to exterminate entire communities, and people at all levels of society were complicit. After the war, Europeans understandably wanted to prevent such atrocities from occurring again. Many countries responded with formal restrictions on the collection of racial data and informal taboos on using race as a concept in social life. Another reason for Europeans' hesitancy to embrace the notion of race is their criticism of US race-conscious policies that legitimize the (supposedly mistaken) notion that biological differences divide the population. In addition, even when Europeans acknowledge that the black-white racial divide is a real social issue in the United States, they claim that cultural differences—that cut across supposed racial categories—are more relevant in European societies. Moreover, European critics claim that because Americans' focus on race reifies the category, it makes it more difficult to fight any racism that does exist.[1]

All of these factors created the tricky situation in which nonwhite ethnic minorities in many European countries could not use race as a basis for political mobilization despite facing racial discrimination that impeded their integration. For decades, this reinforced the poor political integration outcomes for nonwhite ethnic minorities across Europe (Messina 2007). However, there is evidence that things may be changing. France is often considered the European country with the most intense and ideological opposition to using racial categories, and in particular to collecting statistics on racial differences in the population.[2] Yet even in France, there is increasing pressure to find some way of accounting for the experiences of nonwhite ethnic minorities that cannot be reduced to class or national-origin–related factors (Héran 2010; Maxwell 2009; Simon 2010). More broadly, across Europe there is a recognition that long-term racial and ethnic cleavages may be emerging and that something must be done to combat this trend. In part this is because the rise of radical right anti-immigrant parties (like the French National Front and Joerg Haider's Austrian Freedom Party) forced Europeans to become serious about dealing with the divisions. In addition, riots by ethnic minority youth in the British Midlands and France's *banlieues* have provided dramatic examples of the dangers of not addressing racial disadvantages.

Today, in the first part of the twenty-first century, race has gained acceptance as a legitimate, if still controversial, social and political issue in Europe. Even if it is clear that race is not a biological fact but rather a social and cultural construction, it is useful for understanding how racism and discrimination operate (Durkheim 1964). As George Frederickson argues,

> Race . . . is commonly used as a criterion to justify a dominant and privileged position—"accompanied by the notion that 'we' are superior to 'them' and need to be protected from real or imagined threats to our privileged group position that might arise if 'they' were to gain in resources and rights. Here we have 'racism' in the full and unambiguous sense of the term." (quoted in Foner 2005: 12)

This perspective highlights the power relations that influence Europeans' fears of losing cultural homogeneity to nonwhite immigration. Even if Europeans are more willing to speak openly about racial issues, the conversations are not always amenable to ethnic minority political empowerment because of the implicit struggle for how Europe will be defined in the future. For example, one might imagine that Germans' open atonement for the sins of the Holocaust would make them especially sensitive to potential discrimination against contemporary immigrant-origin ethnic minorities. Yet there is a deep reluctance to completely abandon ethnic conceptions of German identity. As Michelle Wright notes, "The Americans, French, and British, to one degree or another, most often pretend to (and to some degree do) overlook race in determining national belonging, instead bringing in a different set of signifiers such as political beliefs, cultural mores, and economic status. . . . Germany, on the other hand, while not prohibiting all non-Germans from becoming citizens, nonetheless has trouble viewing those who do not share a specific racial heritage as 'true' Germans" (Wright 2004: 184–185).

Discrimination directly affects the ability of minorities to participate politically. Although many European countries have only recently begun to grapple with racial discrimination, it became an important issue during the 1980s in the European Parliament (EP), where efforts were made to counteract the influence of racist anti-immigrant political parties who had won seats in the 1986 EP election. Although the parliament itself still has a small number of recognizable ethnic minorities (nine were elected in the 2009 EP election[3]), the EP took the lead in addressing racial violence and antiracism, which led to the Racial Equality Directive in 2000. This type of legislation may eventually impact the ability of ethnic minorities to address discrimination in society and in politics.

Despite legislation like the RED, white European resistance to the growth in ethnic minority political presence will likely continue for the foreseeable future. Even in Britain and the Netherlands, where nonwhite ethnic minorities have the highest levels of political representation in Europe (often equal to the ethnic minority percentage of the population), there are still significant barriers to ethnic minorities' full acceptance in mainstream politics. As subsequent chapters in this book argue, ethnic minority elected officials in both countries are often considered powerless tokens that were chosen by the parties for their symbolic value to concentrated ethnic minority electorates. In addition, despite well-developed sensitivity to multiculturalism and racial difference in both Britain and the Netherlands, those discourses of diversity often marginalize nonwhite communities by not allowing them to operate on the same playing field with mainstream political actors (Duyvendak, Pels, and Rijkschroeff 2009; Small and Solomos 2006: 249–250). Moreover, recent terrorist attacks and the general international political climate have intensified Islamophobia, which some argue is an example of "cultural racism" against Muslims whose values are considered incompatible with European society (Modood 2005). At the same time, immigrant-origin Muslims are increasingly likely to get elected to political office and engage in productive ways with mainstream European politics (Laurence 2012; Modood 2005). All of these trends suggest that the incorporation of nonwhite ethnic minority migrant-origin communities in Europe will remain a central political issue for years to come. This book attempts to make sense of recent developments, by comparing and contrasting political dynamics across a range of countries and examining whether existing academic literature on minority political participation and representation is adequate.

Existing Literature

Academic research on minority political participation in Europe often focuses on why voter turnout rates are lower than among the majority population. One standard explanation is that minority communities often suffer from socioeconomic disadvantages that dampen turnout rates. In addition, migrant minority communities may face cultural barriers that inhibit their full participation in mainstream society. Yet research also suggests that minority and migrant communities can benefit from co-ethnic networks that provide unique resources for political mobilization, at times leading to turnout rates higher than those of the majority population (Cutts et al. 2007; Fennema and Tillie 1999; Leighley and Vedlitz 1999; Maxwell 2010; Messina 2007).[4] The chapters in this volume engage these debates by examining different forms of political participation, including not only mass political behavior but also formal and informal lobbying among minority political activists. This volume also provides a broader perspective on the ways in which minority political participation varies across national contexts. The findings support some of the conventional wisdom but also provoke new ways of understanding minority political participation.

Literature on migrant and minority representation in Europe also tends to start from the empirical baseline of a lack of representation and then analyzes numerous explanations for this dynamic. One of the main insights is that minority communities by definition have small population numbers, and when that is compounded with socioeconomic disadvantages and low participation rates it will be very difficult to obtain significant representation. However, research suggests that different institutional and contextual settings can make those disadvantages more or less easy to overcome (Banducci, Donovan, and Karp 2004; Bird, Saalfield, and Wüst 2010; Gay 2001; Garbaye 2005; Messina 2007; Maxwell 2012). In addition, there are debates about whether descriptive representation (having elected officials who look like their constituents) is necessary for substantive representation, that is, allocating political resources in the best interests of certain constituents (Mansbridge 1999). The chapters in this volume engage research on political representation by providing an overview of the ways in which it varies across specific geographic contexts. Moreover, the chapters suggest that a range of successes and failures are occurring in Western Europe, which provides support for contending perspectives on the opportunities and challenges of minority political representation.

Chapter Overview

In Chapter 2, Jonathan Laurence and Rahsaan Maxwell provide an overview of immigrant incorporation into West European political parties. They argue that the increased salience of immigration has led to two-sided pressures for the diversification of political parties. On the one hand, political parties are increasingly looking to diversify their ranks and developing programs to recruit activists and candidates from different origins. On the other hand, ethnic minority immigrant activists are increasingly organized in their efforts to pressure political parties into diversifying. They consider how these two-sided pressures are creating more opportunities for ethnic minority migrant-origin political actors as well as creating new sources of frustration and tension. One of these sources of frustration is the gap between rhetoric and action among the political party leadership in Europe. They conclude that while minorities now have a foot in the door, increased emphasis on forcing immigrants to assimilate may slow the progress of minority candidates in the future.

James Hampshire's chapter examines the issue of all-black and minority ethnic (BME) shortlists for parliamentary seats in Britain. He argues that a growing consensus on the importance of demand-side obstacles has shifted advocacy from (relatively uncontroversial) proposals for more equality rhetoric and promotion to (more controversial) proposals for equality guarantees such as BME shortlists. However, the 2010 parliamentary election indicates that just as BME shortlists have become more high profile, the need for them may be diminishing.

In Chapter 4, Vincent Geisser and El Yamine Soum provide an in-depth examination of ethnic minority political integration in France. They argue that France has embraced a new rhetoric of diversity and antidiscrimination that purports to offer better prospects for minority integration. However, Geisser and Soum claim that this new rhetoric also leads to new forms of discrimination and ethnic segmentation. In particular, French parties often confine ethnic minority activists to ethnic functions of a lesser value, asking them to be leaders of their supposed communities, while at the same time stigmatizing the notion of a communitarian politics. This limits migrant-origin activists to a devalued ethnic subspace of politics. It also establishes an implicit distinction between "normal elites" and "diversity elites," which renders the latter less legitimate.

Germany's restrictive citizenship laws have created an immigrant-origin electorate that is much smaller than one might expect, as Karen Schönwälder explains in her examination of German minority representation in Chapter 5. She argues that the electoral system, settlement structures, and the lack of group consciousness and mobilization of the immigrant population suggest that the driving forces of immigrant political representation are very different from the situation in the United States and Britain. However, despite being at a relatively low level, the numbers of immigrant representatives have grown significantly over

the past two decades. Yet, for the future, no party has an explicit policy to promote immigrant careers within the organization or to secure
a number of places on candidate lists. She concludes that minority representation is likely to remain low and that growth will come slowly.

The situation in the Netherlands is in sharp contrast to the German
case, as explained in Chapter 6 by Laure Michon. The Netherlands is
one of the few European countries in which the political integration of
non-Western immigrants can be characterized as being successful. In
Parliament, foreign-born members of Parliament (MPs) have been present in significant numbers for twenty years. Similar success can be
found at the local level. In the main cities, Amsterdam and Rotterdam,
some non-Western immigrant groups are even overrepresented on local
councils when compared to their share in the population. However, Michon finds worrying trends in anti-immigrant rhetoric and the high
turnover rate of minority politicians. She argues that while some of the
data presented would point to the successful assimilation of non-Western immigrants into the Dutch political elite, other elements suggest
that non-Western immigrant politicians hold a subordinate position in
Dutch politics. In combination with the change in the public discourse
on integration, and the turn away from multicultural policies, there are
clear challenges for the political integration of non-Western immigrants
in Dutch politics.

In Chapter 7, Terri Givens and Rhonda Evans Case outline developments in antiracism and antidiscrimination policy in the European
Parliament. As Europe moves toward closer integration, EU-level policy plays a greater role in determining the initiatives that will be taken
at the national level in regard to immigrant integration and race relations. The authors describe how the rise of the radical right in countries like France, Germany, and Austria played a key role in moving
forward initiatives like the EU's Racial Equality Directive. The political response to racism was a key factor placing these issues on the
agenda and in the development of policy at the EU level, which is now
in the process of being implemented by member states.

In the conclusion, Martin Schain makes an explicit comparison of
ethnic minority political participation and representation across the four
countries examined in this volume. All too often, political integration
is analyzed from within one nation-state, but Schain highlights the similarities and differences across countries. In addition, Schain places recent European developments in perspective with similar issues in the
United States.

The goal of this book is not to provide definitive answers about the future of ethnic minority migrant political integration in Western Europe. Nor is it to posit a model that would predict successful (or unsuccessful) migrant political integration at all times and in all places. Instead, this book offers careful empirical analysis of recent political developments in four countries and situates them in the broader framework of how race, ethnicity, and immigration are changing European societies. On a theoretical level, the contributions in this book suggest that a combination of national, local, group, and individual-level factors are all relevant for understanding political integration. For example, different national institutions (e.g., electoral systems, nationality law) shape the ways in which migrants relate to the political system. Yet there is also considerable subnational variation according to the political, economic, and social particulars of the local community. Group-level factors are important, as different migrant communities have various types of resources and relationships to the mainstream culture. Yet individual-level factors also shape political outcomes, from educational and occupational attainment to the personality and charisma of an individual candidate. Finally, there is important variation in political integration over time. The most obvious time-related factor is that as migrants acquire citizenship and more familiarity with the host society over time, they will be better able to influence the political system. Yet things do not always improve over time, and the contributions in this volume highlight the importance of contingency and broader political and economic developments that can make integration more difficult for migrant-origin communities. We submit that this book is a helpful guide for anyone seeking to understand the complexities of contemporary political dynamics in Europe.

Notes

1. These contrasting approaches have created significant transatlantic disconnect among academics over the years. For example, Gary Freeman's 1979 book on Britain and France, *Immigrant Labor and Racial Conflict in Industrial Societies* (Princeton: Princeton University Press), was very well received in the United States but highly contested in Europe. Freeman's book tried to chart out the racial and economic aspects of immigration to Europe but critics claimed it was a misguided attempt to import US categories where they did not apply.

2. For more on this debate, see Amiraux and Simon 2006, Simon 1998, or the May 2009 special issue of *Esprit*.

3. Patrick Barkham, "Minority Report," February 14, 2007, www .guardian.co.uk/uk/2007/feb/14/race.eu?INTCMP=SRCH, accessed July 13, 2009.

4. See also the 2004 special issue of the *Journal of Ethnic and Migration Studies*: "Social Capital and Political Integration of Migrants."

2

Political Parties and Diversity in Western Europe

Jonathan Laurence and Rahsaan Maxwell

In this chapter, we explore immigrant incorporation into West European political parties. As more immigrants (and their descendants) obtain citizenship in European countries they have more opportunities to influence electoral politics. In addition, as immigrant communities grow in size (whether as citizens or noncitizens) their needs, interests, and preferences become increasingly important for mainstream political decisions (Bird et al. 2010; Messina 2007). In theory, this should make immigrant communities attractive targets for mobilization by political parties seeking new voters.

Yet, immigrants' new points of access to European domestic politics do not necessarily mean that they will automatically gain clout inside political parties. Immigrant communities tend to have lower voting rates than native-origin communities, which reduces the incentives for political parties to cater to their needs. In addition, much of the current debate around immigrant integration in Europe is focused on the ways in which immigrant communities are problematic. Concerns about terrorism, violent unrest, and a lack of attachment to mainstream society among segregated immigrant communities have led to increased surveillance and skepticism of immigrant political behavior (Caldwell 2009). In addition, the rise of far right-wing parties with anti-immigrant platforms has contributed to the shift toward restrictive and less multicultural policies in many West European countries (Gibson 2002;

Givens 2005; Joppke 2007a, 2007b). All of these trends limit the ability of immigrant actors to advance their careers and their agendas in mainstream European politics.

Despite this backlash against immigrants and their descendants, we argue that two-sided pressures have led to the general diversification of political parties. On the one hand, political parties are increasingly looking to diversify their ranks and are developing programs to recruit activists and candidates from different origins. On the other hand, ethnic minority immigrant activists are increasingly organized in their efforts to pressure political parties into diversifying. We consider how these two-sided pressures are creating more opportunities for immigrant-origin political actors as well as creating new sources of frustration and tension.

Existing Literature on Political Parties and Immigrant Influence

Our analysis of the immigrant-related diversification of political parties supports recent literature on the general diversification of West European political parties as well as literature on the gradual progress of immigrant incorporation. One of the classic perspectives on West European political parties argued that party systems had been "frozen" by societal cleavages from the earlier period of industrialization and universal suffrage (Lipset and Rokkan 1967). These cleavages appeared to produce stable voting coalitions throughout much of the twentieth century, but since the 1970s many scholars have noted a rise in electoral volatility (Mair 1997; Pedersen 1979; Shamir 1984). One explanation for this volatility has been the rise of new "post-materialist" ideological issues for both left- and right-wing voters (Inglehart 1971, 1990). This set of issues created a new axis of party competition, although admittedly with effects that vary cross-nationally according to political institutions (Dalton 1988). The early versions of these arguments focused on issues like environmentalism and feminism, but by the 1980s and 1990s, it became clear that immigration and immigration-related diversity would also influence the party landscape (Messina 1989, 2007).

Although there is general agreement that immigration and immigrant communities are increasingly important for West European electoral politics, there have been debates over the extent of that influence and how it should be evaluated. Classic arguments about immigrant incorporation portrayed the process as something that improved gradually over time (Alba and Nee 2003; Gordon 1964). However, recent research has questioned whether this gradual improvement will apply to recent nonwhite and non-Christian immigrants who may be more prone to stigmatization and find fewer opportunities for upward social mobility in contemporary postindustrial, service-based economies (Caldwell 2009; Portes and Zhou 1993; Sniderman and Haagendoorn 2007). As with many aspects of incorporation, much of the debate over the progress of immigrants' political incorporation depends on whether one focuses on how far immigrants have come or on what remains to be achieved. For example, immigrants are an increasingly important part of West European electorates, but they tend to have lower turnout rates than native-origin individuals. Immigrants are also increasingly represented among European elected officials, but in many cases they are underrepresented relative to their percentage of the population (Bird et al. 2010; Messina 2007: 194–223). To a certain extent, our focus on the dual pressure for diversification elides this debate. We find evidence of gradual improvement in the incorporation of immigrants into West European political parties. However, that incorporation has often occurred in an atmosphere of organized struggle, and the pace and extent of this incorporation is still to be determined.

Pressure from Within: Politicians' Efforts at Diversification via Recruitment

As the immigrant-origin electorate has grown in size, political parties in Europe have tentatively begun outreach to this new pool of voters and activists. One way they have sought to do this is by recruiting promising minority candidates. Most West European countries have increasing numbers of immigrant-origin local councilors, members of Parliament, and in some cases a few cabinet members. However, while the number of immigrant-origin elected and appointed political representatives and members of government is not trivial, it is still modest. This section examines some of the positive developments and ongoing challenges in political parties' efforts to diversify.

As the subsequent chapters in this volume describe in more detail, political leaders across Europe now pay lip service to diversity. This is because almost every party is interested in minorities' votes (even Jean-Marie Le Pen paid a visit to the Parisian banlieue during the 2007 French presidential campaign). Unfortunately the rhetoric does not always match the reality. The ironic underside of Cem Özdemir's victory in fall 2008 as Green Party chairman in Germany, the first German of Turkish origin to win such a position, was his absence from a good position on the parliamentary candidate slate from his political base in Baden Württemberg. Similarly, the appointment of Malek Boutih as national secretary for social affairs of the French Socialist Party in 2003 was a landmark event. But even though Boutih would appear to be made of parliamentary timber, his party never took the practical steps to get him elected. Some immigrant-origin commentators have noted acrimoniously the gap between rhetoric and action among the French Socialist leadership. An editorial on a Muslim community website published after Barack Obama's victory in November 2008 targeted one white French Socialist politician who "cried upon hearing the beautiful news" but who did not object to being "parachuted" by party leadership into a minority-heavy electoral district outside of Paris after losing her parliamentary seat elsewhere.[1] And she did so without hesitating to take the place, in the words of the journalist, of all "Mamadous and Fatimas" in the neighborhood who might have represented their district themselves.

Very few individuals of visible minority background have gained access to elite leadership positions or electable positions on party ballots. At present, a structural obstacle of clubby and risk-averse party machines confronts minority candidates of all socioeconomic backgrounds—even well-connected wealthy entrepreneurs or individuals with the right diplomas. To date, one-half century into the historic post–World War II settlement of tens of millions of people of color, only a handful of such individuals have risen into Europe's political elite.[2] This underrepresentation is partly the legacy of earlier obstacles to naturalization that led a high percentage of adult immigrants to retain their original citizenship. But it also reflects a youthful population. If one excludes minors from the European immigrant population, a relatively small number of majority-age citizens (approximately one-third) remains. This is too small and diverse of a group of voters to constitute a swing electorate that might compel party leadership to diversify their ranks with more alacrity.

The small number of individual politicians of minority background who have entered the fray of national politics and the recentness of enfranchised citizens of immigrant origin means it is wise to avoid sweeping generalizations on this topic at this early stage. However, some general trends are increasingly evident, and the remainder of this section presents some brief examples of recent developments among political party actors in France and Germany.

France

In France, where the political class prides itself on a color-blind approach to minority integration, the number of non-European-origin elected officials is extremely small. Table 2.1 provides a rough overview of the number of non-European-origin elected officials across several levels of government in 2004 and 2008. To place the data from Table 2.1 in perspective, recent research indicates that non-European-origin immigrant communities are roughly 10 percent of the metropolitan French population (Maxwell 2012). This significant underrepresentation suggests that party leaders believe there is little to be gained by promoting minority candidates (Lagrange et al. 2009). Moreover, when political parties do field minority candidates, they are often in unwinnable districts. The percentage of successful non-European-origin candidates in a recent election was only 8.71 percent in the Socialist Party and 3.44

Table 2.1   French Elected Officeholders of Non-European Origin

	2004	2008	Total
Parliamentary deputy	0	1	577
Senator	2	4	321
European Parliament deputy	3	n/a	77
Regional councilor	44	n/a	1,719
Municipal councilor	1,069 (3.18%)	1,844 (6.68%)	142,000
General councilor (cantons)	32	n/a	3,804

Sources: "Elus d'origine non-européenne en France métropolitaine" [Elected officials of non-European origin in metropolitan France], Suffrage universel (http://users.skynet.be /suffrage-universel/fr/frmiel.htm); Malika Ahmed, "Les arabes et le référendum" [Arabs and the referendum], May 18, 2005 (www.sezame.info); Tabet 2009.

Note: In 2008, an additional 495 French elected officeholders of non-European origin were deputies to the mayor, and 4 were mayors. Haut Conseil à l'intégration study relied on a survey of surnames in cities with more than 9,000 residents.

percent in the governing Union for a Popular Movement (UMP) party (Tabet 2009).

Nonetheless, there have been small signs of progress. Some parties have made explicit promises to increase the number of candidates of immigrant origin. To address the representative deficit, Martine Aubry, who was elected first secretary of the French Socialist Party in 2008, announced her intention to put "visible minorities" in 20 percent of the party's elected positions. President Nicolas Sarkozy even threatened to cut the subsidies of political parties who do not expand the diversity of their candidate pool. These efforts have already yielded results. In 2002, there were 123 "diversity" candidates out of 8,000 running for Parliament in the first round of elections (Laurence and Vaïsse 2006). In 2008 municipal elections, political parties nominated 2,000 such candidates out of 520,000 total candidates (Fournier 2008). In smaller cities, visible minority candidates for city councils accounted for as many as 6 to 7 percent of the total number of politicians up for consideration by the electorate, but only half of these candidates were listed high enough on the ballot to actually have a competitive chance at being elected. The most minority candidates were put up for election by the centrist Mouvement Démocrate (MoDem, Democratic Movement), followed by the Socialist Party, the governing UMP, assorted Left tickets, and the Green Party (Fournier 2008). Each major party (MoDem, UMP, Socialist) had at least one minority candidate heading up an electoral list in 2010's regional elections, in which only 100 "visible minority" politicians were fielded across France.

Yet these milestones appear modest when one considers that there is only a single black member of the National Assembly from metropolitan France (George Pau-Langevin, a Socialist from Paris), who won a hard-fought election in 2007. There are a total of seventeen black members of the lower house of Parliament (i.e., 3 percent), but the other sixteen of them hail from France's overseas territories and domains (Dom-Tom). Four senators of North African origin have been seated by political parties (the French Senate is indirectly elected) (Vaïsse 2009).

One of the most significant obstacles to achieving a "representative" sampling of political elites in France is the lack of precise population data. Without reliable data on the size of various immigrant-origin groups, it can be difficult to make a case for promoting greater representation. To address this issue, in 2008 President Sarkozy appointed Yazid Sabeg as Diversity and Equal Opportunities Commissioner. In 2009, Sabeg proposed a series of reforms that would fundamentally change the way France categorizes and promotes ethnic minorities.[3] The proposals stopped short of revolutionizing the census or imposing quotas on political parties—both goals that the commissioner had earlier supported—but they did mark a forceful policy agenda in the context of French political culture: reserving space in preparatory classes for Grandes Écoles, an apprenticeship quota in all companies with more than fifty employees, and a busing policy to desegregate schools. If France were to engage in further new endeavors that went beyond simple "antidiscrimination" measures—such as aiming for "parity" or concrete goals in terms of the number of visible minorities on parties' candidate lists—this would mark a quantum leap for the participation of visible minority candidates in political life.

Germany

Germany also has a long way to go in addressing the issue of minority candidates. Although some children of immigrants have joined political parties and other civil society organizations in Germany, they remain a lonely few. A handful of naturalized Turkish Germans have made their way up in local and national politics, including visible positions in the Bundestag (though none has yet joined a government cabinet) (Laurence 2007). A small but significant core of party members from Turkish and Muslim backgrounds have become elected officials in local, national, and European parliaments. Cem Özdemir (B90/Greens), a member of the European Parliament, served two terms in the Bundestag (1994–2002). He was the first German of Turkish origin to reach national office, as well as the first to become chairman of a national political party. As the most prominent non-European-origin politician, he could one day hold a high position in German government.

The Seventeenth Bundestag (2009–2014) includes five members of Turkish origin and one of Iranian origin: Lale Akgün (Social Democratic Party, SPD, Cologne), a psychologist who earlier worked for immigration offices in North Rhine–Westphalia; Ekin Deligöz (B90/Greens, Bavaria), a Bundestag member since 1998; Omid Nouripour (B90/Greens, Hessen), who took over as representative of Joschka Fischer's former constituency in 2006; Hakkı Keskin (Left Party/Linkspartei, Berlin), a community college instructor and immigrant activist who was an SPD member until 2005; Sevim Dagdelen (Left Party/Linkspartei, North Rhine–Westphalia), who had a career as a journalist; and Hüseyin-Kenan Aydin (Left Party/Linkspartei, North Rhine–Westphalia), a former trade union leader from IG Metall. German parties also have sent at least four deputies of Turkish origin to the European Parliament: Cem Özdemir (B90/Greens); Ozan Ceyhun (SPD), who led a national get-out-the-vote effort for his party in 2002; Vural Öger (SPD), an entrepreneur who served on the government's immigration commission in 2000; and İsmail Ertuğ, an SPD member and local mosque federation spokesman in Hamburg. In addition, several young Turkish Germans hold national-level party positions and are visible participants in national political debates, such as Bülent Arslan (Christian Democratic Union, CDU), who is leader of his party's German-Turkish Forum (DTF); Giyasettin Sayan, a spokeswoman for the Left Party; Emine Demirbüken-Wegner (CDU), who was a longtime local foreigners' commissioner in Berlin; and Mehmet Daimagüler (Free Democratic Party, FDP), a former member of his party's executive board. These individuals who participate in national debates are complemented by a handful of local officials in Land-level parliaments. Aygul Özkan (CDU) made headlines in 2010 when she became the first Turkish-origin state-level minister in North Rhine–Westphalia.

This rising class of immigrant-origin politicians suggests that political parties have become more aware of the potential boon that the minority-origin constituency represents. Moreover, this constituency is likely to grow considerably in the future. Although the political parties' response is still primarily symbolic, it suggests an attempt to establish recruitment patterns that will serve them well in the future.

Pressure from Without: Immigrant Efforts at Diversification

Political party elites are not the only actors driving these recent changes. Immigrant activists have become increasingly organized and vigilant about pressuring party elites to support new candidates. There are three main types of pressure that these activists have pursued. One is formal organization inside political parties to develop structured factions that push for better positions for immigrant-origin candidates. A second pressure is informal lobbying from influential immigrant politicians who have already achieved some power. A third strategy consists of grassroots mobilization and rallying more candidates and voters from outside the party structure to generate new influence.

Formal Organization

In order to pursue the strategy of formal organization inside political parties, migrant communities must have a critical mass of well-established party activists. This has been most common in Britain and France, where immigrant communities arrived relatively soon after World War II and faced the fewest restrictions to citizenship (Garbaye 2005). Due to the early arrival and automatic British citizenship for many immigrants, immigrant pressure groups within political parties started in Britain in the early 1980s with the Labour Party Black Sections. These developments have been slower to arrive in other countries, but in the past decade immigrant-origin political activists have become increasingly organized within their political parties.

In Britain, the 1970s was a decade of intense community organization among ethnic minority immigrants as they struggled to improve their schools, fight against police brutality, and obtain support from local councils for projects (e.g., cultural centers or religious celebrations) that mattered to their communities. This mobilization coincided with increased voting participation and the first wave of ethnic-minority immigrant municipal councilors in Britain was elected during the 1970s, primarily to the Labour Party (Le Lohé 1998). Yet, by the early 1980s, many of these activists became frustrated by the slow political process and their lack of influence within the party power structures. In response, a broad coalition of ethnic minority immigrant Labour Party members created the Labour Party Black Sections (LPBS) in 1983 (Sewell 1993; Shukra 1998a).

The LPBS was supposed to provide a forum within the Labour Party for "black" (a term that at the time referred to all nonwhite ethnic minorities in Britain) activists to share their concerns and pressure the party elites into supporting their agenda and their candidates. Immigrant-origin activists complained that party elites were exploiting blacks for their votes and not giving them any real influence, so this was seen as a way of obtaining that influence (Sewell 1993; Shukra 1998a). At the time there were several organized sections within the Labour Party that represented different constituencies (e.g., women, young people, or trade unionists). However, the national Labour Party leadership refused to recognize the LPBS on the grounds that it would promote segregation and "apartheid" within the party (Anwar 1986: 119). This pushed the struggle to the local level where activists across the country attempted to establish black sections in their local Labour Party organization, with mixed success. The fight for LPBS autonomy also overlapped with other divisions in the party as LPBS supporters tended to be on the left wing of the party. This gave the LPBS added leverage because during the 1980s the left wing of the Labour Party was particularly strong and party elites often had to accept their demands in order to maintain a united Labour front against electoral challengers (Shukra 1998b: 119–120; Solomos and Back 1995: 76–90).

The 1987 general election is often considered the culmination of the LPBS struggle because four nonwhite ethnic minority candidates were elected members of Parliament. This was a significant step forward because it catapulted nonwhite politicians onto the national stage and most likely would not have happened as quickly without LPBS pressure (Sewell 1993; Shukra 1998a). Although nonwhite ethnic minorities in Britain remain underrepresented relative to their percentage of the population in most political offices, they have made continual progress since 1987 with increasing numbers of elected and appointed individuals. After the 2010 general election, nonwhite ethnic minorities in Britain were roughly 8 percent of the overall population but 3.7 percent of the House of Commons, 5.4 percent of the House of Lords, and 5.5 percent of the members of the European Parliament. As seen in the country-specific chapters in this book, there are very few countries with significant numbers of nonwhite immigrant-origin members of Parliament, and only the Netherlands comes close to the levels of proportional representation achieved in Britain (Messina 2007). Moreover, on the municipal level the outcomes are even better, and some ethnic groups (most notably South Asians) are often overrepresented on municipal councils in cities with significant nonwhite communities (Maxwell 2012).

The growth in immigrant-origin politicians in Britain is not solely a function of the LPBS. Yet, the formal pressure from inside the party was an important strategy that helped transition ethnic minority candidates from a mainly local stage into national politics. After 1987, the local black sections lost momentum as the Labour Party began to lose control of local councils (which had always been an essential power base for the LPBS movement). In addition, Labour shifted to the center in the 1990s, and a new wave of more moderate nonwhite politicians began their ascension (Shukra 1998b: 121–124). Nonetheless, the LPBS movement stands out as an early example of how immigrant communities in Western Europe could organize inside political parties to push for better representation of their interests.

The LPBS movement is well documented, but less is known about similar dynamics that have occurred inside French political parties over the past decade. For various reasons (most notably the timing of migration and different citizenship policies), immigrant politics in France has tended to lag behind developments in Britain by about ten years (Garbaye 2005). Therefore, while immigrant politicians were first elected to municipal office in Britain during the late 1970s and 1980s, that did not begin to happen in France until the 1990s. Much like the LPBS in Britain, when these internal pressure groups have emerged in France they have focused on expanding the influence of immigrant-origin candidates beyond the municipal to the national level.

Among the West European countries who were the first to receive migrants after World War II (most notably the four countries examined in this volume), France stands out as having some of the most trenchant barriers to immigrant political influence. Nonwhite ethnic minority groups in Britain and the Netherlands are almost proportionately represented relative to their percentage of the populations among members of Parliament, and Turkish people in Germany are not far away. In comparison, there is only one nonwhite immigrant-origin member of Parliament in metropolitan France, and she was elected in 2007. Often, this gap is attributed to the dominant assimilationist discourse in France which delegitimizes the concept of ethnic communities and punishes political actors who attempt to represent ethnic minority interests (Geisser 1997). In addition, recent research has argued that in the conservative French political culture it is difficult for all political newcomers (whether women, young people, or ethnic minorities) to gain influence. In particular, the lack of term limits, the *cumul des mandats* (accumulation of seats) system in which individual politicians can hold several elected positions at the same time, and the centralized way in which many of the electoral lists are chosen make it very difficult for newcomers to gain leverage over the political process (Geisser and Soum 2008).

Into this environment, internal political pressure groups emerged in the early 2000s. They were organized by immigrant-origin activists who had been engaged in the political parties for several decades and had begun to get elected to municipal councils but were not seeing many of their immigrant-origin colleagues in positions of power or as viable parliamentary candidates. Due to France's assimilationist discourse, these pressure groups kept a much lower public profile than in Britain and activists did not always seek official recognition from the central party leaders.[4] Nonetheless, before each election, groups of activists began privately lobbying leaders to increase the diversity of candidates. In some cases, activists had formed semi-official factions within the parties that presented unified policy platforms and attempted to recruit as many party activists to their cause as possible.[5] However, these efforts never got very far because such actions were quickly labeled "communitarian," stigmatized as dangerous to the French status quo, and few party activists would support the efforts. Even when such factions did not explicitly focus on ethnic or immigrant-related issues, if there were too many nonwhites in the group, they were often stigmatized. According to a young sub-Saharan African-origin activist in the Green Party:

> I created a group with a lot of black people. But it wasn't about black people. We wrote a platform about equality, environmental issues, 3rd world solidarity, and we got 6% of votes [in the internal party primary]. We tried to leverage that into positions on the list but we got called communitarian and shut down. People still mention that and label me that way so I avoid all talk of forming any kind of group![6]

By most accounts, the internal pressure groups in French political parties have not been as successful as their British Labour Party counterparts (Equy and Inzaurralde 2007; Libération 2007). Yet while immigrant-origin activists in France are still waiting for a dramatic breakthrough, there has been slower incremental progress, especially on the municipal and regional councilor levels (Maxwell 2012). Moreover, the pressure groups inside French political parties are part of a larger trend toward more high-profile immigrant-origin "clubs" and "reflection circles" that have attracted successful professionals to the cause of increasing diversity in French power structures.[7] Unlike the immigrant organizations from the 1980s and 1990s that were based in disadvantaged ghettos, these new organizations have become prominent by using elites to argue that more diversity is needed. Although progress may not be as fast as in other countries, there is evidence that French political parties are changing and slowly responding to the diverse constellation of interests in contemporary society (Olivier 2003).

In Germany, a country that has traditionally limited the political rights of immigrants, nearly all German political parties now have a subsection with hundreds of members that seeks to recruit citizens of immigrant origin to their respective platforms. For example, the Arab Social Democrats (Arabische Sozialdemokraten, A-SPD) in Berlin; the Greens have Immigrün; the CDU has the German-Turkish Forum (Deutsch-türkisches Forum); and, finally, the FDP set up a Liberal German-Turkish group (Liberale Deutsch-Türkische Vereinigung). These bodies were established by minority members of the parties as a way of signaling their respective parties' friendliness to voters with an immigrant background. These members also serve as the de facto spokespeople for their parties on integration issues (and at times on unrelated matters such as foreign policy, the economy, or the environment). These German developments are only embryonic in comparison to Britain but are much more robust than those in France.

Informal Lobbying

A more informal strategy for immigrant-origin activists to gain better positions within political parties is to use personal connections and influence. There is evidence that immigrant-origin activists are increasingly present in elite circles where they can leverage these types of connections. While immigrant-origin individuals may not yet be the most powerful constituency in West European politics, they are nonetheless making progress.

Personal connections and influence can be most useful in systems with high party control over candidate selection, where internal negotiations are more important than private funding or primary votes. In France, the political parties are infamous for their backroom negotiations and for the central party structure being able to impose candidates on local constituencies (Borella 1990). This dynamic has often worked against immigrant-origin candidates who lacked significant connections within the parties and were placed on party lists in ineligible positions. This was seen as a way of attracting votes from local minority communities without actually empowering the immigrant-origin candidates (Geisser and Soum 2008). Yet to the extent that immigrant-origin activists can leverage connections to their advantage, it increases their visibility and chances for success.

The 2007 election of George Pau-Langevin as the first immigrant-origin nonwhite deputy in metropolitan France was a prime example of how powerful connections are useful for advancing a candidacy. Pau-Langevin was born in Guadeloupe but migrated to metropolitan France for her studies and had been an activist with the Socialist Party (PS) since the 1970s. When the Socialists took control of the Paris Mayor's Office in 2001, Pau-Langevin was appointed General Delegate for the Affairs of Residents from the Overseas Departments, which raised her profile and allowed her to establish more high-level contacts.[8] For the 2007 campaign, Pau-Langevin's candidacy for the Twenty-First District in Paris was supported by a crew of PS heavyweights (including Bertrand Delanoë, Dominique Strauss Khan, and Victorin Lurel) against the incumbent Socialist deputy Michel Charzat.

It was a rare occurrence for the party to support a new candidate against an incumbent, but it was downright remarkable to support a new black Caribbean woman against a well-established white man. A subtext of the campaign was that the incumbent Charzat was part of Laurent Fabius's PS faction and the leader of the PS, François Hollande, wanted to nominate someone from his own faction, which ended up being Pau-Langevin. Charzat tried to block Pau-Langevin's candidacy, complained that she was being "parachuted" in from outside the constituency, and pushed for a partywide vote on the matter. In response, Pau-Langevin's high-level allies lobbied harder for her candidacy and managed to approve her nomination without a vote.[9] None of this would have been possible without high-level advocates. For example, Lurel threatened to quit his position as the PS national secretary for overseas departments if Pau-Langevin was not chosen (Salin 2007). In the end, Pau-Langevin prevailed and her historic candidacy was successful.

Pau-Langevin's personal connections obtained over several decades of activism were useful for taking her career to a higher level, but such connections can also help start a career. Janine Maurice-Bellay is a Caribbean-origin woman who never finished high school but was elected regional councilor for the Île-de-France in 2004. In her case, a chance meeting with PS deputy Claude Bartolone sparked her interest in politics. At the time, Maurice-Bellay was working for a hospital in a job she did not particularly like. Bartolone happened to be visiting the hospital and was present for an argument between Maurice-Bellay and her boss. Bartolone was so impressed with Maurice-Bellay's comportment that he asked her to work for him in the PS. Bartolone was then an important mentor for Maurice-Bellay as she learned about politics and prepared to become a candidate. Bartolone was in the Fabius faction so Maurice-Bellay knew she would face internal opposition from the dominant Hollande faction. But, in 2004 when she prepared to run for regional councilor, she benefited from strategic support from the informal association of black activists that was pushing to get more black people elected.[10] Maurice-Bellay also benefited from the personal influence of Lurel, who lobbied Hollande on her behalf much as he would do a few years later for Pau-Langevin.[11]

Pau-Langevin and Maurice-Bellay are not unique among politicians in the sense that personal connections are often important for forming and advancing careers. Yet, to the extent that such connections are now possible for immigrant-origin politicians in Europe, it is evidence that immigrant-origin individuals are becoming increasingly integrated into the fabric of European political life and political parties. Similar stories and dynamics apply to other immigrant-origin politicians in Europe and are evidence that these growing networks may benefit larger numbers of immigrant-origin individuals in the future (Geisser 1997; Michon 2007).

Grassroots Mobilization

A third strategy for immigrant-origin candidates is to rely on grassroots mobilization. Existing research suggests that this strategy may be most successful in single-member district electoral systems where the community in question lives in areas with high residential segregation and therefore will have more demographic influence in the elections (Barreto, Segura, and Woods 2004; Bird 2003; Trounstine and Valdini 2008). This may explain why the strategy of grassroots electoral mobilization has been most effective among Pakistanis and Bangladeshis in Britain. Pakistanis and Bangladeshis in Britain have high levels of residential segregation and British politicians are elected to single-member districts. However, there is evidence of variants on this strategy elsewhere in Western Europe.

As mentioned earlier, immigrant-origin individuals in Britain have been relatively successful at getting elected to office. Pakistanis and Bangladeshis have been especially successful on municipal councils in Britain where they are often overrepresented relative to their percentage of the population in large cities and cities with large ethnic minority populations (Le Lohé 1998; Maxwell 2012). There are several dynamics that have contributed to this success, including Pakistani and Bangladeshi turnout rates for local elections that are higher than those of all other ethnic groups (including native British whites) (Purdham et al. 2002). In addition, the ability of community leaders to mobilize this high turnout and channel it toward particular candidates or parties has wielded significant influence over election outcomes and the overall balance of power on numerous municipal councils in Britain (Garbaye 2005: 141–142; Muir 2005; Saggar 1998a: 64; Saggar 1997: 693–707).

Pakistanis and Bangladeshis have also used this electoral mobilization to influence candidate selection and the promotion of politicians from within their community. The British Labour Party candidate selection process for local elections is relatively transparent and local party organizations hold much of the power. If specific constituencies can fill the room during candidate selection meetings, they can control the process. Bangladeshis and Pakistanis have proven especially adept at this strategy and at times have been able to control over 75 percent of the votes in these meetings, allowing them to nominate their own candidates. The high levels of Pakistani and Bangladeshi turnout then helped ensure that the candidates would be elected (Garbaye 2005: 137–138; Geddes 1998; Solomos and Back 1995: 101). This strategy allowed Pakistanis and Bangladeshis to enter new candidates into the political process who did not have long-standing connections with the party elites but who could mobilize their own community as a base of support. The success of this model of grassroots mobilization has established a new power structure for South Asians in British politics because many local Labour chapters increasingly rely on the South Asian political machine for controlling local councils.[12]

France's conservative political culture has generally made it difficult for minority communities to mobilize their own grassroots constituencies. However, the two-round electoral system provides an opportunity for smaller parties to use their vote score in the first round to negotiate with major parties for inclusion on the second-round ballot in a position of higher influence than they would otherwise have received. Various communities of immigrant origin (Maghrebian, Caribbean, Sephardic Jewish) have used this strategy to demonstrate their electoral importance and get elected in cities where they were previously locked out of the municipal council (Garbaye 2005: 207–209; Maxwell 2012). In many respects, this has been a more effective form of applying pressure on French political parties than the formal groups of activists organizing within individual parties.

Yet there are risks associated with this strategy in France, especially given the public taboo on ethnic community organization and the potential for stigmatization of such an approach. While an ethnically oriented list may be able to mobilize members of that particular ethnic community, it risks offending the broader public and stirring up resentment among voters and politicians who do not find ethnic identities a legitimate basis for political organization. In addition, younger immigrant-origin activists have complained that they get branded as "too ambitious" if they try to organize their own list and become proactive about their political future, so they risk having their advancement within the party blocked as a result.[13] There are opportunities for well-mobilized communities in France to force their influence onto the electoral process. However, given the conservative nature of the overall political-party power structure, it remains difficult for immigrant-origin communities in France to mobilize without some mainstream allies.

Conclusion

Political parties in Western Europe are slowly but surely becoming more diverse and incorporating more immigrant-origin individuals. This chapter has shown that a two-sided pressure, both from political parties seeking to reach out to new voters and from immigrant-origin activists demanding their place, is changing West European politics. The details and the specific dynamics vary across countries, but the trend is occurring across the Continent.

Although this chapter has focused on the similarities among Britain, France, and Germany, it is important to note that cross-national institutional differences are also relevant for how party diversification occurs. The combination of single-member district elections and relatively high levels of ethnic residential segregation in Britain allow for unique immigrant leverage in the candidate selection process. Moreover, high turnout rates (and high residential segregation) among South Asians in Britain have made them especially attractive as candidates in local elections where victory can come down to a handful of votes (Maxwell 2012). In France, the party list system used for most elections concentrates more power in the party elites and has made it difficult for outsiders like migrants to obtain leverage. Moreover, France's conservative political system makes it difficult for new groups of any kind (ethnic, racial, gender, religious, age) to obtain access to elected office (Bird 2005). Another significant institutional difference is the relative ease (or difficulty) of obtaining citizenship. Germany has long had some of the more restrictive laws concerning access to citizenship for immigrants and their descendants (Brubaker 1992). Those laws have been liberalized over time, but the overall citizenship acquisition rates for non-European-origin immigrant communities tend to be lower than in Britain and France, which reduces the likelihood of these communities being able to exert electoral influence. There are also important differences between Britain and France on this issue as British nationality laws allowed colonial and former colonial subjects who migrated prior to 1962 to access citizenship as soon as they arrived. This facilitated earlier political participation than in France where many immigrants did not become citizens until the second or third generation (Garbaye 2005). Our overall argument in this chapter is that similar trends of party diversification are occurring across Western Europe, but we also acknowledge the variety of ways in which that trend develops.

Although the general trend points toward increasing diversification within West European political parties, we have also highlighted the significant challenges to providing more comprehensive influence for immigrant-origin communities. There are entrenched and powerful constituencies in many of the main parties that do not see outreach to new immigrant-origin communities as being in their best interest. In some respects this is baffling because research on voter identification suggests that party preferences among immigrants and immigrant-origin individuals in Western Europe skew heavily leftward (Messina 2007). Yet, many of these immigrants (in particular Muslims) hold political views that are socially conservative. This suggests an opportunity for center-right parties to make inroads into immigrant-origin communities. However, many politicians on the right fear that fielding minority candidates or conducting public outreach to minority voters may lead to reduced support from the native right-wing base, which could outweigh the benefits of attracting immigrant voters. In addition, immigrant-origin communities tend to have lower turnout rates. Moreover, immigrant-origin communities in Europe are often concentrated in a limited number of electoral districts. This makes it possible for parties to craft localized appeals with ethnic minority candidates in the specific districts with large immigrant communities but not necessarily incorporate more immigrant-origin politicians into the broader party structure. Finally, the recent shift toward a renewed emphasis on assimilation and restrictive citizenship may further marginalize immigrant interests. Yet, immigrant communities now have their foot in the door across most political parties in Western Europe, which was not the case during previous decades. How quickly this opening gets wedged into further political influence remains to be seen.

Notes

1. Mourad Ghazli, "Pas d'Obeurmania dans les partis," Oumma TV, 2008, www.oummatv.tv/Pas-d-Obeurmania-dans-les-partis.
2. For an excellent study of Muslim elites in Europe, see Klausen 2005.

3. Yazid Sabeg, "Programme d'action et recommandations pour la diversité et l'égalité des chances," May 2009, www.premier-ministre.gouv.fr/IMG/pdf /Rapport_Commissariat_diversite.pdf.

4. One prominent exception is the Cercle de la Diversité Republicaine (CDR). CDR is an organization inside of the center-right UMP and has been very public about its goals to increase diversity within its political party. This appears to break some of the standard French taboos but is in line with recent developments among Sarkozy and the UMP, who seem more prepared to explicitly address issues of ethnic and religious diversity than their center-left Socialist counterparts (Laurence 2009). For more see www.cercle-diversite.org/site.

5. Although this chapter draws a connection between French political party pressure groups and the British LPBS, there is evidence that ethnic minority political mobilization in the United States may have been more of a direct influence for many of the actors in France (Gabizon 2008).

6. Interview with Eros Sana, June 5, 2009.

7. Examples include Africagora, Club Averroes, Club XXIème Siècle, and the Conseil représentatif des associations noires de France (CRAN).

8. Interview with George Pau-Langevin, December 27, 2004, Paris.

9. Interview with PS official, July 2006, Paris.

10. After the 2004 election, this group became formally known as Africadom. Africadom continued mobilizing for a few years within the PS but became significantly weaker after the election of George Pau-Langevin. Africadom had been hoping to present its own list of candidates for various elections but Pau-Langevin's election as deputy was portrayed by some in the PS as having used up all the political capital for the case of ethnic minority immigrant-origin candidates, at least for the time being.

11. Interview with Janine Maurice-Bellay, August 1, 2006, Paris.

12. It is worth noting that it remains to be seen how viable this strategy will be in the long term. Much of the Pakistani and Bangladeshi influence is based on being able to guarantee consistent turnout in local elections with relatively low turnout and therefore relatively slim margins of victory (often fewer than 100 votes). Pakistanis and Bangladeshis may be highly concentrated in some electoral wards, but their electoral success has spread beyond those few as a result of the effective vote mobilization networks. However, in wards where Pakistanis and Bangladeshis are currently overrepresented relative to their population size they could be vulnerable to the emergence of organized voting blocs from other communities. Moreover, to the extent that Pakistanis and Bangladeshis begin to assimilate and live in more mixed neighborhoods, this model of group mobilization may be less feasible.

13. Interviews with Sabri Haddad, PS activist, June 9, 2009, and with Eros Sana, Green Party activist, June 5, 2009.

3

Race and Representation: The BME Shortlist Debates in Britain

James Hampshire

In an interview with *The Times* newspaper shortly after the election of Barack Obama as president of the United States, Trevor Phillips, chair of the UK Equality and Human Rights Commission, reflected on the improbability of a black prime minister. No stranger to controversy, Phillips claimed that the reason this was so unlikely had less to do with British public attitudes than the machinery of party politics: "Here, the problem is not the electorate, the problem is the machine. . . . The parties and the unions and the think-tanks are all very happy to sign up to the general idea of advancing the cause of minorities but in practice they would like somebody else to do the business. It's institutional racism" (quoted in Thomson and Sylvester 2008). Despite this indictment, Phillips went on to reject the idea of using all-black and minority ethnic (BME) shortlists for parliamentary seats as a way of breaking the deadlock, preferring softer forms of positive action such as a special funding for potential BME candidates: "any positive action has to be based on giving people who are already competent a bit of an edge" (Thomson and Sylvester 2008).

As one of the leading voices for racial equality in the UK, Phillips's ambivalent stance on positive action is significant in itself. But it also serves as a useful barometer for the state of the debate on the representation of ethnic minorities in British politics. In recent years, a number of race-equality groups and senior politicians have argued that the persistent underrepresentation of ethnic minorities in Parliament requires new legislation to allow "harder" positive-action measures. In particular, they have argued that the use of all-women shortlists by the Labour Party to select parliamentary candidates for the 1997 and 2005 elections should be replicated for BME applicants. For proponents of BME shortlists, only by requiring party selectors to choose from a constrained list will Parliament come to embody a diverse range of members of Parliament (MPs); for opponents, BME shortlists would provoke a disastrous racialization of electoral politics and undermine meritocratic selection in the name of political correctness.

This chapter explores the political debates around the representation of ethnic minorities in Parliament and the proposals for BME shortlists. It is structured as follows: The first section provides the empirical context for debates about BME shortlists, providing background data on the representation of ethnic minorities in the British Parliament. The second section considers factors that might explain BME underrepresentation, using a supply- and demand-side model, before discussing the implications that the various factors have for strategies to improve representation. Drawing on Lovenduski's (2005) typology of equality strategies, it is argued that a growing consensus on the importance of demand-side obstacles has shifted advocacy from (relatively uncontroversial) proposals for more equality rhetoric and promotion to (more controversial) proposals for equality guarantees such as BME shortlists. The third section then outlines the institutional context in which the debate about BME shortlists has unfolded, showing how the race relations paradigm, the Westminster parliamentary system, and the party system shape representational politics. The fourth section considers the recent political debates about how to tackle underrepresentation, showing how the use of all-women shortlists by the Labour Party led to calls for similar measures to increase the number of BME MPs. The fifth, concluding section considers what the 2010 election results mean for the BME shortlists debate. It is argued that just as BME shortlists have acquired increased profile, the need for them may in fact be diminishing.

Trends in BME Representation in Parliament

BME representation at Parliament goes back further than is sometimes assumed. The first nonwhite member of Parliament was elected as early as the mid-nineteenth century. David Ochterlony Dyce Sombre, of mixed English and Indian descent, won the seat of Sudbury for the Radical-Liberals in 1841, only to be removed in 1842 following allegations of bribery during the election campaign. In the later nineteenth and early twentieth century, three Indians were elected to the House of Commons. Dadabhai Naoroji served as Liberal MP for Finsbury Central from 1892 to 1895; Mancherjee Bhownagree ran for the Conservatives in 1895, winning Bethnal Green North-East which he represented until 1905; and Shapurji Saklatvala represented Battersea North for Labour from 1922 to 1923, and then as a Communist from 1924 to 1929 (Smith 2008: 3). Thus, well before colonial immigration transformed the ethnic makeup of British society in the post–World War II years, the British Parliament included a few visible minorities.

However, during the postwar decades, minorities were conspicuous by their absence, despite the fact that there were no legal obstacles to Commonwealth immigrants standing for Parliament.[1] Indeed, it was not until 1987 that the first BME MPs of the postwar era were elected. The class of 1987, all Labour MPs, were Diane Abbott (Hackney North and Stoke Newington), Paul Boateng (Brent South), Bernie Grant (Tottenham), and Keith Vaz (Leicester East).

As Table 3.1 shows, since 1987 the number of BME MPs has increased. The general trend is clearly upward, with increases in the total number of BME MPs at each election since that breakthrough. Yet progress has been slow, and although there is now a record twenty-six

Table 3.1 Number of Ethnic Minority MPs by Party, UK General Elections, 1979–2010

Year	Conservative	Labour	Liberal Democrat[a]	Other
1979	0	0	0	0
1983	0	0	0	0
1987	0	4	0	0
1992	1	5	0	0
1997	0	9	0	0
2001	0	12	0	0
2005	2	13	0	0
2010	11	15	0	0

Note: a. Social Democratic Party (SDP)–Liberal Alliance for 1983 and 1987, the Liberal Party for 1979.

BME MPs (of which eight are women), this is still well short of the number required if Parliament were to mirror the ethnic composition of wider British society. The total population of the UK is just under 62 million, with the BME population estimated to be about 11 percent of the total.[2] Assuming these figures to be correct, for the ethnic composition of Parliament to reflect the wider population there would need to be about 71 BME MPs (the total number of MPs after the 2010 election is 650).

This concept of representativeness, sometimes referred to as descriptive representation, is not without its critics. Yet over the past decade or so it has become increasingly accepted by political elites that the underrepresentation by BME MPs as compared to the size of BME communities in the wider population is a problem of considerable urgency. The basic logic is quite simple: as the former Labour government minister Alan Johnson put it in a speech to the Labour Party Ethnic Minorities Forum, "if 10% of Britain is black and minority ethnic then we ought to expect a similar percentage in our democratic structures."[3] The election of Barack Obama only reinforced these debates, as a number of commentators pondered whether a "British Obama" could have found success in Westminster politics.

In addition to simple numerical underrepresentation, there are at least two further aspects of the BME presence in Parliament that merit attention: first, the partisan politics of BME representation; and second, the spatial distribution of BME MPs.

Up until 2010 the overwhelming majority of BME MPs were members of the Labour Party. This partly reflects underlying socioeconomic and regional voting patterns: ethnic minorities are disproportionately located in the socioeconomic groups and urban areas that have traditionally supported Labour. But it also reflects the fact that since the 1960s Labour has pursued more BME-friendly policies, most obviously race-relations legislation,[4] and has therefore been widely seen as the party of ethnic minorities. Until very recently, the Conservatives, by contrast, had not made many efforts to engage with BME communities. The upshot is that Labour has historically received about 80 percent of the ethnic minority vote (Anwar 1994; Saggar 1998b), and aspiring politicians from BME backgrounds have mostly pursued careers through the Labour Party. As discussed later in the chapter, the 2010 results indicate a shift in some of these patterns.

The second important feature of ethnic minority political representation, and indeed recruitment, in Britain is its territorial circumscription. What the raw numbers in Table 3.1 do not show is that historically nearly all of the BME MPs have represented constituencies with large BME populations. As Saggar and Geddes (2000) argue, debates about BME representation are racialized in the double sense that race or ethnicity is seen to "matter" only in contests for seats with large BME communities and, moreover, BME candidates are only likely to be selected for such seats. In contrast to debates about the underrepresentation of women, the geographical concentration of minorities, combined with a "color-coding" of parliamentary seats, has sometimes pushed race to the margins of British politics. Under this logic, party managers and elites have directed minority representation claims toward constituencies with relatively large ethnic minority populations—ethnic minority candidates for so-called "ethnic minority seats" (Nixon 1998)—while such matters are seen as largely irrelevant for the rest of the population. Thus "the politics of race and ethnicity have assumed something of a ghetto status on the contemporary political landscape" (Saggar and Geddes 2000: 26).

To summarize, despite steady increases in the number of BME MPs since 1987, as well as a substantial increase in the number of Conservative BME MPs in the 2010 election (more of which later), ethnic minorities are underrepresented in the British Parliament. There would be almost three times more BME MPs if their presence in Parliament were to reflect the relative size of BME communities in the population as a whole.

Explaining the Underrepresentation of Ethnic Minorities

What explains this underrepresentation of ethnic minorities? This question can be usefully approached by distinguishing between the supply- and demand-side factors that shape political recruitment (Norris and Lovenduski 1995; Geddes 2001). This approach holds that the outcome of selection processes is shaped by "the interaction between the supply of applicants wishing to pursue a political career and the demands of selectors who choose candidates on the basis of their preferences and perceptions of abilities, qualifications and perceived electability" (Childs et al. 2005: 23).

On the supply side, there are a number of factors that may explain why ethnic minorities, as well as people from other underrepresented groups such as women, may not put themselves forward as potential candidates. Supply-side barriers act to prevent or deter people from applying for selection or even forming an aspiration to apply. They include the monetary costs of standing for office, the time commitment required, cultural factors, lack of confidence, and lack of aspiration caused by few role models (House of Commons 2010: 110). For example, financial barriers may impact disproportionately on women and ethnic minorities who are more likely to work in lower paid sectors of the economy. The time commitment required to campaign for a seat may deter women with child-care responsibilities and those in jobs without flexible working arrangements. Persons from some ethnic and cultural backgrounds may face opposition from other members of their community if they say they want to stand, or they may lack the confidence to put themselves forward in the first place. These supply-side factors can combine to form compound barriers or disincentives; thus, a mother of ethnic minority background may face multiple obstacles to applying for selection.

Demand-side factors include discrimination within political parties as well as institutional constraints associated with political structures of the party system and British race politics. The most obvious demand-side explanation of underrepresentation is racial discrimination on the part of selectorates within political parties. This may take three forms: explicit, implicit, or imputed racism. Explicit racism in selection processes occurs when BME applicants face overt discrimination from party members. Implicit or indirect discrimination occurs when BME applicants are disadvantaged because they do not conform to preconceived ideas about what constitutes a good MP (the white, middle-class male stereotype). Finally, imputed racism occurs when party members believe that racism in the electorate at large will undermine the party's chances of success if they select a BME candidate. This is sometimes known as the electoral liability thesis, the assumption that BME candidates face an ethnic penalty that undermines their electability. It is difficult to prove that this is at work, though there have been some high-profile examples where BME candidates have performed much worse than expected, and this was put down in part to their ethnicity: the large swing against Labour candidate Paul Boateng in Hertfordshire West in 1983 and the defeat of Conservative candidate John Taylor in Cheltenham in 1992 are two well-known examples.

A second set of demand-side factors relate to institutional constraints of the electoral system and British race politics (Geddes 2001). The phenomenon of "color-coding" ethnic minority candidates for "ethnic minority seats," mentioned earlier, is relevant here. A "representational idiom" (Geddes 2001) in which it is assumed that BME candidates are most "appropriate" for seats with large BME populations limits the number of potential seats ethnic minorities could stand for. Until very recently, it has certainly been the case that BME candidates were mostly selected only for winnable seats with substantial ethnic minority populations; where they were selected to contest seats without sizeable BME populations, these constituencies tended not to be winnable for the party in question. This racial coding is built upon and reinforces the liability thesis, and it creates an inherent limit to the number of seats BME applicants stand a realistic prospect of being selected for. Combined with an electoral system with a low turnover (only a handful of seats that are winnable for any given party typically become vacant in any one electoral cycle), this coding has meant that the "demand" for BME candidates has typically been concentrated on a small number of constituencies.

The relative explanatory value of the various supply- and demand-side factors, as well as their *perceived* explanatory value, has significant implications for the strategies that political parties and other actors are likely to use to increase the representation of underrepresented groups. We can see this by drawing on a typology developed by Joni Lovenduski, which outlines three basic strategies for increasing the diversity of parliamentary candidates: equality rhetoric, equality promotion, and equality guarantees (Lovenduski 2005; Childs, Lovenduski, and Campbell 2005). Equality rhetoric refers to discursive commitments made by parties and political leaders to increase the diversity of representatives, for example, through speeches, campaign platforms, and party literature. The aim of this strategy is to affect the attitudes and beliefs of both aspirant candidates and party selectorates, thereby stimulating both the supply and demand for applicants from underrepresented groups. Equality promotion consists of measures aimed at bringing those who are currently underrepresented into political competition, for example, through mentoring schemes, financial assistance, or targets. The aim here is to boost the supply of applicants by increasing their resources, skills, and motivation. Lastly, equality guarantees require an increase in the number or proportion of candidates with a particular characteristic (e.g., sex or ethnicity) and are achieved through mechanisms such as quotas, reserved shortlists, or reserved seats. This is the most interventionist, and often controversial, strategy as it effectively aims to create artificial demand (though it may secondarily also increase supply). All-women and all-BME shortlists are forms of equality guarantees as they ensure that a woman or BME applicant is selected as the parliamentary candidate for a party that adopts them in a given constituency. They stop short of a parliamentary quota (i.e., a requirement that a certain percentage of MPs should be of a given characteristic) but are likely to increase the number of MPs with that characteristic, especially if used by parties in winnable seats.

Addressing the supply-side factors behind underrepresentation implies a mix of equality rhetoric and equality promotion. Both strategies have been used by the major parties in recent years. All of the three main party leaders have made discursive commitments to increasing the diversity of their candidates, and their parties have reinforced this with a number of equality promotion initiatives (examples are discussed below).

However, while supply-side barriers are important, researchers (e.g., Childs, Lovenduski, and Campbell 2005; Saggar 2001) and campaigning organizations such as the Fawcett Society and Operation Black Vote have increasingly argued that demand-side barriers are the greater obstacle to increasing representation of women and ethnic minorities. They argue that underrepresentation is explained not so much by a lack of BME or female candidates putting themselves forward for selection as a lack of demand by political parties for such candidates. If demand-side obstacles are indeed the main reason why more BME applicants are not being selected, then the third strategy, equality guarantees, are likely to be advocated. Although equality rhetoric and promotion may increase the supply of applicants, relatively few of these applicants will be selected and put before the electorate if discrimination (direct, indirect, or imputed) or color-coding in a context of low seat turnover are at play. In particular, the willingness, or lack thereof, to select BME candidates by local party selection panels in winnable constituencies (many of which will be without substantial ethnic minority populations) cannot be addressed through supply-side measures. Therefore, to significantly increase the selection of BME candidates for a given party's winnable seats would require demand-side measures.

In short, while an explanation of the underrepresentation of ethnic minorities in Parliament requires attention to both demand- and supply-side factors, there is a growing belief that some of the most significant obstacles are on the demand side, particularly around the selection process. Certainly this is the view of BME campaigners, including Trevor Phillips, quoted above as identifying the problem within the party machine, and the leading advocacy group Operation Black Vote, which argues that "whether by design or default party political selection processes have held back BME individuals" (OBV 2008: 2.5). This has motivated advocacy for equality guarantees, particularly BME shortlists.

Equality Guarantees and the Race Relations Paradigm

In some ways the debates about BME shortlists in Britain mirror wider debates about positive or affirmative action in North America and Europe. However, the call for BME shortlists is particular to the institutional context of British race politics and the way this intersects with the structures of British representative democracy. In Britain, public policy discourse about race and ethnicity is inevitably couched in terms of "race relations." Race relations can be thought of as a policy paradigm, as defined by Peter Hall: "a framework of ideas and standards that specifies not only the goals of policy and the kind of instruments that can be used to attain them, but also the very nature of the problems they are meant to be addressing" (Hall 1993: 279). The development of the race-relations paradigm dates back to the 1960s, when the Labour government of Harold Wilson developed antidiscrimination legislation as a progressive quid pro quo for restrictive immigration legislation (Hampshire 2006).[5] It remains very much prevalent to this day. Two aspects of the race-relations paradigm are relevant to understanding the politics of BME shortlists: its ambivalent legitimation of racial identification and its legal framework for positive action.

The race-relations paradigm is ambivalent about racial identification because it normalizes and legitimizes racial categories as ascriptive identities, but at the same time delimits their normative significance and the extent to which they can be used as the basis of differential treatment. On the one hand, the very idea of "race relations" presupposes the validity of race as a category since it postulates relations between racial groups and therefore bestows legitimacy on the idea of racial identities (Hampshire 2009). Unlike several other European countries where race is not commonly used in public discourse (e.g., Germany) or is refused as a basis for categorization (e.g., France), in Britain, race is widely referred to in official language and policy, albeit for purposes of antiracism.[6] This sits rather uneasily alongside a meritocratic color-blind discourse, which denies that race should be a factor in selection decisions and is skeptical about measures targeted at particular racial or ethnic groups. The effect is that "race undoubtedly commands an unusually strong degree of conceptual legitimacy in British policy and party circles, though—curiously—at the price of restricting its underlying penetration of thinking and practice" (Saggar and Geddes 2000: 38). This ambivalence seeps into the debates about BME shortlists because it provides legitimacy to the categories (e.g., black, Asian, BME, etc.) that would underpin equality guarantees but also gives a discursive resource to those who oppose using racial categories for the purpose of positive action.

This ambivalence is also reflected in the legal framework associated with race relations. Prior to the passage of the 2010 Equality Act, which unified various aspects of equality and antidiscrimination law, the 1976 Race Relations Act was the legal basis for tackling discrimination based on race or ethnicity. Under this legislation, some limited forms of "positive action" were allowed, including targeted training or "encouraging only persons of a particular racial group" to apply for work or training (Race Relations Act 1976, Part VI, 37(1) b). The 2010 Equality Act extends this logic, allowing targeted measures to prevent or compensate for disadvantage faced by persons who share a "protected characteristic," which includes race, sex, disability, and sexual orientation (Equality Act 2010, Chapter 2, 158–159). Thus, under the race relations and antidiscrimination laws, equality rhetoric and promotion that is targeted at particular groups is perfectly legal. However, neither the previous Race Relations laws nor the new Equality Act permit equality guarantees such as reserved shortlists or quotas. Under existing legislation, BME shortlists would be illegal, as indeed were all-women shortlists until the Labour government passed the 2002 Sex Discrimination (Election Candidates) Act to exempt the candidate selection procedures of political parties from aspects of the sex-discrimination laws.

These ideational and legal dimensions of the race-relations paradigm intersect with two wider institutional features of British representative politics to shape the shortlists debate: the parliamentary system of government and the party system. To an outside observer the focus on Parliament might seem rather narrow. Why should debates about the underrepresentation of ethnic minorities in public life focus on this institution? While there are undoubtedly other areas of public life in which ethnic minorities are underrepresented, the legislature has a particular importance in Britain due to the parliamentary system of government, in which the government is drawn from the legislature. The majority of ministerial posts are held by MPs, and the head of the government, the prime minister, must by convention be an MP. Thus the route to high office is almost exclusively through Parliament. This means that getting selected and elected as an MP is an essential part of any aspiring politician's career strategy; hence the importance of Parliament for representation more broadly.[7] For there to be a "British Obama," there must be British BME MPs.

The second feature of British representative politics that shapes strategies to increase the representation of BME MPs is the party system, in particular the role of party procedures and internal party dynamics on the selection of candidates. In the Westminster Parliament, most MPs represent one of the major parties (in the 2010 Parliament, 622 out of 650 MPs, 95.6 percent, were members of one of the three major parties), with the remainder being members of the nationalist parties and a few smaller parties. There are very few independents. Furthermore, UK voters tend to vote along party lines rather than for a particular candidate (indeed voters often do not know much about the candidate chosen by their preferred party). This means that parties act as gatekeepers to public office, and their selection procedures are fundamental in shaping the type of applicants who are put before the electorate. These procedures rarely employ US-style primaries for the selection of candidates.[8] While each of the parties has its own rules, in general the local party associations play a key role in selecting candidates. Indeed, in an era of centralized campaign planning and management, this is the one power that local parties retain. This can, and in many cases has, created tensions between the central party office, which may wish to impose a particular candidate or set of candidates, and local party members. For example, as discussed later, both the Labour Party's all-women shortlists and the Conservatives' "A-list" met with opposition from local party members who (correctly) saw them as attempts to reduce their autonomy in selecting candidates. This is particularly significant for the selection of BME candidates because it has been suggested that while senior politicians and party managers are generally committed to addressing the issue of BME underrepresentation—in their rhetoric at least—attitudes among local party members may not be so conducive. Thus, equality rhetoric by party leaders and even equality promotion coordinated by central party offices may be insufficient if party members are not supportive of the strategy. A belief that this is the case is one of the arguments behind BME shortlists as a form of equality guarantee.

Tackling Underrepresentation— From Equality Rhetoric to Equality Guarantees?

Until recently, attempts to increase BME representation in Parliament were predominantly a matter of internal Labour Party politics. As mentioned previously, the majority of ethnic minorities voted for Labour, and the party was seen as far more responsive to ethnic minority concerns, as shown by the successive antidiscrimination laws passed by Labour governments. During the 1980s, the main BME initiative within the Labour Party was a form of self-organized equality promotion known as the Black Sections movement (see the discussion in Chapter 2 of this volume by Laurence and Maxwell as well as Shukra 1998a; Solomos and Back 1991; Geddes 1995). The Black Sections movement was strongly associated with the left wing of the party, however, and was not recognized by the party leadership. When the party moved to the center during the mid-1980s, the Black Sections movement was further marginalized. Although it had succeeded as a vehicle for the promotion of the four BME MPs who were elected in 1987, it was clear that a more thoroughgoing transformation required the issue of underrepresentation to be taken up by the party leadership and, moreover, by a party in government. So long as the Conservatives held power further progress seemed a distant prospect.

The landslide victory for Labour in 1997 was therefore highly significant. Nine BME Labour MPs were elected, almost double the previous number. Moreover, with Labour in power the chance of a government equality strategy was substantially increased. The first of Lovenduski's three aspects of equality strategy, equality rhetoric, came immediately and from the very top. At his first party conference speech as prime minister in 1997, Tony Blair signaled the new mood: "We cannot be a beacon to the world unless the talents of all the people shine through. Not one black High Court judge; not one black Chief Constable or Permanent Secretary; not one black army officer above the rank of colonel. Not one Asian either. Not a record of pride for the British establishment. Not a record of pride for Parliament, that there are so few black and Asian MPs."[9]

The Conservatives drifted further to the right during the first Labour term, and the inclusion of women and ethnic minorities was not made a priority under the leadership of Iain Duncan Smith. In 2002, the first female Conservative Party chairman, Theresa May, warned a stunned party conference that they had come to be perceived as the "nasty party" by many voters. This was the beginning of an attempt to claw back the center ground from Labour. David Cameron's election as leader in 2005 ushered in a modernizing rhetoric, reminiscent of Blair's challenges to the Labour Party in the mid-1990s. As part of a decontamination strategy, the Conservative Party made a concerted attempt to move away from its narrow, "nasty" image. Embracing a more diverse range of candidates was central to this rebranding. In a speech given in Leeds on December 12, 2005, less than a week after he had won the leadership contest, David Cameron announced a five-point plan to increase the diversity of Conservative MPs, using language that was a world away from his predecessors:

> When I launched my leadership campaign I said that our Party had to change fundamentally. . . . crucially, [by] broadening our representation in Parliament so we better reflect the country we aspire to govern. . . . When it comes to black and minority ethnic MPs, there are so few in my Party that it's as easy to name them as count them, so here goes: Adam Afriyie and Shailesh Vara. . . . We need people from diverse backgrounds to inform everything we do, to give us the benefit of their diverse experience, to ensure that we stay in touch with the reality of life in Britain today. Only if we engage the whole country in our Party will our Party develop ideas that benefit the whole country. . . . By changing the face and the faces of the Conservative Party, I believe we will increase the number of people in this country who listen to what we have to say.[10]

The Liberal Democrat leader, Nick Clegg, whose party has never had a BME MP, has not made diversification such a central part of his leadership strategy. But he too has upped his equality rhetoric, for example, saying at a 2008 Manchester event to raise money for Liberal Democrat campaigns against the far-right British National Party that "I want the Liberal Democrats to be a party that represents the whole of Britain. We simply cannot represent modern Britain until modern Britain is represented in us."[11]

At the same time that equality rhetoric has burgeoned, the main parties have all launched equality promotion initiatives. The Labour Party launched a Black and Ethnic Minority Forum at the 2004 Annual Conference and then relaunched the dormant Black Socialist Society in 2006. The Conservatives launched their "five-point positive action plan" to increase the number of women and BME MPs, which included a mentoring project as well as the controversial priority list (A-list) of parliamentary candidates (discussed in the next section). The Liberal Democrat Party set up the Ethnic Minority Liberal Democrats in 2001, to organize "recruitment and training and promote ethnic minority members towards greater involvement in the political processes of the party."[12] In 2006, they also created a £200,000 "fighting fund" for women and BME candidates running in target seats.

Yet despite the increase in equality rhetoric and promotion within the parties, the relatively slow pace of change during the 2001 and 2005 parliaments led to growing calls from BME campaigners and a few MPs for the adoption of equality guarantees to increase the number of BME MPs. This was catalyzed by the Labour Party's decision to use precisely such measures to increase the number of women MPs. Labour had used all-women shortlists to select candidates for half of their winnable seats in the 1997 election, which contributed to a large increase in the number of women MPs (a total of 120, or 18.2 percent of all MPs, 101 of whom were Labour MPs). All-women shortlists were, however, deeply controversial and were successfully challenged in the courts (Rentoul et al 1996). Neither the Conservatives nor the Liberal Democrats supported a change in the law to allow all-women shortlists, and for the 2001 election Labour did not use them. However, following the reduction of women MPs to 118 in 2001, the government legislated to allow all-women shortlists with the 2002 Sex Discrimination (Election Candidates) Act. In 2005, they were used again by Labour and the number of women MPs increased to 128, or 19.8 percent of all MPs.

The use of all-women shortlists created a precedent for group-specific selection procedures: if equality guarantees in the form of all-women shortlists were a suitable method to increase underrepresentation of women, why not for BME underrepresentation, which shared many similar demand-side obstacles? Shouldn't the "logic of positive action" (Geddes 1995) naturally extend to BME shortlists? The precedent set by all-women shortlists was certainly used by campaigners for a BME equivalent. For example, when the leading BME advocacy group, Operation Black Vote, made the case for BME shortlists in their 2008 report for the Government Equalities Office, they were explicit that their proposals "would emulate the path Government took when they made political parties exempt from the provisions within the Sex Discrimination Act relating to the selection of election candidates" (OBV 2008: 1.10).

During 2007–2008, the Labour government seriously considered making such an exemption. The context was the proposed Equality Bill, which was intended to unify and simplify the various antidiscrimination and equalities laws. Consultations on the bill began in June 2007 when the Discrimination Law Review published a consultation paper entitled "A Framework for Fairness: Proposals for a Single Equality Bill for Great Britain." For a brief period it looked as though an enabling clause to allow (though not require) political parties to use BME shortlists would be included in the bill. The equalities minister, Harriet Harman, was supportive and in 2007 she commissioned Operation Black Vote to write a report with proposals about how to improve BME representation. The report was published in May 2008 and, unsurprisingly, advocated legislation to allow BME shortlists (OBV 2008). However, in the time while it was being prepared, several leading politicians, both inside and outside the Labour Party, came out strongly against such a move. This included not only the usual suspects in the Conservative Party and right-wing commentariat, but also some BME MPs, notably Sadiq Khan and Khalid Mahmood, who said that the proposal "smacks of a colonial attitude" and would be "a form of political apartheid which will encourage division and segregation,"[13] and some Labour-affiliated organizations such as the Fabian Society, whose director, Sunder Katwala, was openly critical (see Katwala 2008). A few supportive BME MPs tried to rescue the idea, notably Keith Vaz, one of the class of 1987 and now chairman of the Home Affairs Select Committee, who tabled a Private Member's Bill to allow shortlists on February 6, 2008. But the opposition from leading BME figures combined with a wider lack of consensus proved fatal.

By early 2008, the government had decided against including provisions for BME shortlists in the Equality Bill. The very possibility of shortlists had stirred up a controversy and the government did not want to jeopardize the other parts of the Equality Bill around which there was more of a consensus. It was not helped by the fact that the OBV report had been delayed and contained some rather unconvincing arguments, for example, suggesting that improving parliamentary representation would help to tackle Muslim extremism. In its official response to the Equality Bill consultation, the government said it would extend positive action by allowing employers to take "underrepresentation of disadvantaged groups" into account when selecting between equally qualified candidates, and it would extend the permission to use women-only shortlists for selection of parliamentary candidates to 2030. However, it explicitly stated that it would not legislate to allow for BME shortlists but would pursue "nonlegislative measures" to increase the political representation of ethnic minorities at the national and local levels (HMSO 2008); in other words, equality promotion, not equality guarantees.

The debate about BME shortlists did not end there, however. In a separate development, Parliament had established its own investigation into issues of representation. In November 2008, the Speaker of the House of Commons, Michael Martin, launched a Speaker's Conference on Parliamentary Representation with a remit to "consider, and make recommendations for rectifying, the disparity between the representation of women, ethnic minorities and disabled people in the House of Commons and their representation in the UK population at large" (House of Commons 2010). Consisting of a cross-party membership of MPs, Speaker's Conferences are a rarely used device to investigate constitutional issues that would need wide support to address. Previous conferences had recommended the enfranchisement of women (1916–1917) and votes for eighteen year olds (1960s), both of which were subsequently adopted. The Speaker's Conference on Parliamentary Representation sat throughout 2009, taking evidence (including from the three main party leaders) and holding public meetings. Its final report was published in January 2010. The report presents three arguments for widening the representation of "individuals from all sections of society" in the House of Commons: justice, effectiveness, and enhanced legitimacy. It made numerous recommendations, including a recommendation in favor of BME shortlists: making a direct comparison to all-women shortlists, the report says that "equivalent legislation should now be enacted to allow political parties, if they so choose, to use all-BME shortlists" (House of Commons 2010: Section 149). Presenting the report to an adjournment debate in Westminster Hall on March 30, 2010, Anne Begg MP, vice-chair of the Speaker's Conference, insisted on the importance of a diverse Parliament: "it's an imperative. . . . The fact is that, in most cases, it remains more difficult for a candidate who does not fit the 'white, male middle-class' norm to be selected, particularly if the seat is considered winnable. Our recommendations are aimed at putting that right, and we hope this debate will highlight the need for government, political parties and Parliament to implement these changes."[14] The report was presented so close to the 2010 election that it got rather lost in the media coverage of the impending campaign. Furthermore, the chances of its recommendations being implemented would rest with the new Parliament and coalition government.

The 2010 Result and the Future of BME Shortlists

It is likely that the 2010 result will have important repercussions for debates about the representation of ethnic minorities in Parliament, and therefore for proposals for the adoption of BME shortlists. As Table 3.1 shows, in 2010 the number of BME MPs almost doubled (from fifteen to twenty-six MPs) and, even more significantly, the number of BME Conservative MPs increased more than fivefold (from two to eleven MPs). Even if the increase in the total number of seats won by the Conservatives in 2010 as compared to 2005 is taken into account, the change is still remarkable: the party has gone from having BME MPs comprise just 1 percent of its total MPs to 3.6 percent. True, this is still well below the number of ethnic minorities in the population at large, but it is nevertheless a major change. The Conservative breakthrough is also notable for its impact on the spatial distribution of BME MPs. Several of the newly elected BME Conservatives represent constituencies with relatively small ethnic minority populations, which may indicate a weakening of the "color-coding" referred to earlier, under which the major parties had tended only to field BME candidates in seats with sizeable BME populations. With several Conservative BME MPs now representing constituencies with predominantly white populations, this may be coming to an end.

In the short-term these changes will surely dampen, if not completely snuff out, calls for the Conservative-Liberal coalition to take immediate measures on underrepresentation, such as those recommended by the Speaker's Conference. In the medium-term, it may indicate a trend toward wider inclusion across the main parties that will obviate the need for BME shortlists altogether. While the Conservative result is undoubtedly more spectacular, it is also worth noting that the increase from thirteen to fifteen MPs for the Labour Party continues a trend of gradual increase since 1987, and moreover, in the context of a substantial loss of total seats for the party. In fact, the percentage of Labour MPs who are BMEs has increased from 3.65 to 5.81 percent.[15] In short, both of the main parties have recorded an increase in total and percentage of BME MPs. The glaring exception here is the Liberal Democrats, who continue a long-standing tradition of having not a single BME MP. Nevertheless, the wider trend is clear: the total proportion of BME MPs in Parliament has increased from 2.3 percent in the 2005 Parliament to 4 percent in the 2010 Parliament.

Moreover, the increase in BME MPs in 2010 was achieved without the use of equality guarantees, suggesting that existing measures of equality rhetoric and, above all, equality promotion may be working. The unprecedented increase in Conservative BME MPs was achieved using a method that stopped short of all-BME shortlists, known as the priority list or A-list, which is legal under current antidiscrimination legislation. The A-list consisted of a centrally compiled list of applicants seeking to stand as Conservative parliamentary candidates. The list was at the core of David Cameron's action plan to diversify the Conservative parliamentary party and included more than half women applicants and smaller, though still substantial, numbers of ethnic minorities. The original rules for the A-list, announced in May 2006, required local parties in target seats and currently held seats to select from the list, although in "exceptional circumstances" they would be able to choose a local candidate. It was deeply unpopular with parts of the party, especially at the grassroots where many members resented what they saw as central office's attempt to impose candidates on them. From the perspective of increasing the number of BME candidates, it was an unequivocal success. Several BME candidates were selected through this method, often in winnable seats, and of the nine new Conservative BME MPs elected in 2010, six had been on the A-list.[16]

This would suggest that "hard" positive action measures such as BME shortlists are not necessary to increase BME representation. In fact, as the Fabian Society argued in their campaign against the introduction of BME shortlists, the wider trends in candidate selection suggest that for the 2010 cohort of candidates the "ethnic penalty" may be diminishing across the board. Research conducted by Sunder Katwala showed that not only did the major parties select more BME candidates for the 2010 election, they were also increasingly selecting them to contest winnable seats.[17] The Labour Party selected BME candidates for 10.5 percent of *all* new selections, and 15.4 percent of selections in seats currently held but with a new candidate. In other words, in the safest Labour seats BME applicants were overrepresented compared to their size of the population as a whole. For the Conservatives a similar pattern held, with the percentage for all BME selections at 4.9 percent, and 9.4 percent for currently held seats. Only the Liberal Democrats were not selecting proportionately more BME candidates in safe seats as compared to total selections (indeed, the Liberal Democrats did not select a single BME candidate in a currently held seat and only one in a target seat, which they failed to win).

In conclusion, it seems that the need for BME shortlists may have diminished at precisely the time when they have gained most attention. Even prior to 2010, the proposals foundered due to a lack of consensus within the Labour government. Today, the evidence on trends in candidate selection, the increase in BME MPs, plus the advent of a Conservative-led coalition government that is much less receptive to arguments for equality guarantees all reduce the likelihood that BME shortlists will be adopted. Of course, there is no guarantee that the increase in BME representation will be repeated at the next election. But if equality promotion of the kind used by the Conservatives yields anything close to the 2010 result and the wider trends in selection of BME candidates continues, then the need for BME shortlists would be seriously undermined. While it may be a long time yet before a "British Obama" emerges, it seems unlikely that he (or indeed she) will have come to office via a BME shortlist.

Notes

1. Then, as now, citizens (then subjects) of colonial and Commonwealth countries could vote and stand for election to the British Parliament.

2. These figures are estimates as the 2001 census is now outdated. The figures from the most recent census, 2011, are not yet available. The total population figure is based on the National Statistics Office Mid-2009 population estimates, while the BME population estimate is taken from their 2008 population estimates by ethnic group. See www.statistics.gov.uk/statbase/Product .asp?vlnk=15106.

3. Alan Johnson, "Race, New Labour and Politics," speech to the Labour Party Ethnic Minorities forum, 2007. The text of the speech can be found at www.thenewblackmagazine.com/view.aspx?index=646.

4. Every major piece of antidiscrimination legislation in Britain has been passed by a Labour government: the 1965 Race Relations Act, the 1968 Race Relations Act, the 1976 Race Relations Act, the 2000 Race Relations (Amendment) Act, and most recently the 2010 Equality Act.

5. It is important to note that due to Britain's imperial citizenship regime the political integration of colonial and postcolonial immigrants has followed a very different trajectory to many other European countries where the focus of debate has and in some cases continues to be about citizenship. In the UK, citizenship was a nonissue. Most immigrants had full citizenship rights, including the right to vote and stand for Parliament. Therefore, they did not face the legal obstacles of naturalization as a precondition of political participation. See Hansen 2000; Hampshire 2005.

6. Although note that the 2000 European Race Equality Directive has prompted an increase in antiracist race talk and some limited convergence on antiracism policies across Europe.

7. Some ministerial posts are held by appointed members of the House of Lords, and indeed some of these have been held by prominent BME politicians, notably Baroness Scotland (Labour, attorney general, 2007–2010), Baroness Amos (Labour, leader of the House of Lords, 2003–2007, and briefly secretary

of state for international development, 2003), and Baroness Warsi (Conservative, minister without portfolio, 2010–). Nevertheless, it remains true that the vast majority and certainly all of the most senior ministerial posts (prime minister, chancellor of the exchequer, foreign secretary, and home secretary) are appointed from among elected MPs.

8. The Conservative Party has experimented with open primaries in a few constituencies, though sometimes with controversial results. In Bethnal Green and Bow, the local party association did not endorse the candidate selected by local residents at an open primary held in March 2009. Despite these experiments, open primaries are not likely to become a widespread selection method.

9. Prime Minister Tony Blair's Speech to the Labour Party Conference, Brighton, September 30, 1997. Accessed at www.prnewswire.co.uk/cgi/news /release?id=47983.

10. Speech by David Cameron, December 12, 2005, accessed at www.conservatives.com/News/Speeches/2005/12/Cameron_Until_were _represented_by_men_and_women_in_the_country_we_wont_be_half_the _party_we_could_be.aspx.

11. See "Nick Clegg Calls for More Diversity in the Liberal Democrats," February 22, 2008, www.ethnic-minority.libdems.org/news/000005/nick_clegg _calls_for_more_diversity_in_the_liberal_democrats.html.

12. For more see www.ethnic-minority.libdems.org.

13. Quoted in Andrew Grice, "Black Shortlists 'Would Create Political Apartheid,'" *The Independent*, March 27, 2008. Accessed at www.independent .co.uk/news/uk/politics/black-shortlists-would-create-political-apartheid -801230.html.

14. "MPs to Debate Representation in Commons," March 29, 2010, www .parliament.uk/business/news/2010/03/mps-to-debate-representation-in -commons/.

15. From 13 out of 356 Labour MPs in the 2005 election to 15 out of 258 Labour MPs in the 2010 election.

16. Correspondence with Conservative Party official. July 12, 2010.

17. See "Black and Asian MP Candidates No Longer Face Race Penalty," www.fabians.org.uk/media/press-releases/mps-ethnicity. The subsequent percentages are also taken from here.

4

The Legacies of Colonialism: Migrant-Origin Minorities in French Politics

Vincent Geisser and El Yamine Soum

In this chapter we explore whether current developments in the French debates around diversity and antidiscrimination policies have led to substantive political changes. Until recently, French political institutions refused to take specific measures that would promote the integration of African, Maghrebi, and Caribbean migrants of postcolonial origin.[1] Any strategies that directly targeted the issue of racial or ethnic discrimination were considered hostile to the French republican tradition. Moreover, these approaches were often caricatured as typical of Anglo-Saxon societies where minority communities form intractable and segregated ghettos. In France, the onus was on migrants to integrate because there were no special government programs to address their migrant-specific needs, which supposedly created incentives for better assimilation (Schnapper 1991).

This French republican logic framed minorities' assimilation as a test of their ability and merit. If citizens of migrant origin were not successfully integrated, it was due to their inability to adapt to French society. Minorities were also expected to become fully French before influencing politics or holding a position of power within the political parties. In many respects, this evoked colonial-era treatment when the indigenous populations were excluded from full citizenship because of their supposed lack of maturity (Taraud 2008).[2] To access French citizenship, colonized people were required to demonstrate their capacity for higher development by forsaking their cultural and religious heritage (Bancel, Blanchard, and Vergès 2003).

Today, the descendants of postcolonial migrants no longer have a separate legal status. On paper, those who acquired French nationality benefit from exactly the same political rights as other citizens, such as the right to vote and eligibility for all elections. There is no legal obstacle to their political participation. However, one of the biggest limitations has been the contradictory expectation that minority candidates simultaneously be assimilated French republicans and representatives of their ethnic-origin group (Geisser 2006).

For example, in Goussainville, a city north of Paris, an independent list of candidates known as Engaged Generation (Génération Engagée) took part in the municipal elections of 2008 under the leadership of Demba Sokhona. Engaged Generation received 14 percent of the first round vote, which should have given them significant negotiating power in the second round. However, politicians from the larger Socialist Party criticized Engaged Generation for being too focused on their ethnic origins. Within the French republican system, this allowed the Socialist Party to marginalize Engaged Generation, even as they included candidates from Engaged Generation in the second round of voting in order to win more seats. Yet despite the supposedly abstract and not ethnically-specific values that the Socialists claimed to defend, they placed candidates from the Engaged Generation list in charge of youth programs, urban policy, and culture, issues that were considered appropriate for candidates of migrant origin. This example shows how politicians can easily adopt an ultrarepublican discourse while at the same time participating in ethnicized practices. Moreover, when postcolonial minorities are forced into positions that supposedly represent their community it is often less about political recognition and more about minimizing their role in the broader political system (Geisser 1997). This inferior status has traditionally been justified by the concept of republican integration because political actors with migrant origins are seen as minors who must prove their assimilation before they can share equal responsibilities with the other French politicians.

However, in recent years there is evidence that a countervailing trend may be undercutting the traditional French republican values. In the late 1990s, the struggle against discrimination finally became an official part of the French political agenda (Fassin 2002). This recognition was timid and mainly due to pressure from European institutions that forced France to adopt a law and establish an institution that would combat gender, ethnic, racial, and religious discrimination. Nonetheless, for the first time, France had to admit that the problems faced by citizens of postcolonial origin are not exclusively due to their poor social and cultural integration but also because of racism. This conceptual mini-revolution means that all mainstream parties on the left and the right now officially place the struggle against discrimination as one of their highest priorities.

All republican political parties (except for those of the Far Right) now engage in symbolic competition for promoting diversity and leading the fight against ethnic, racial, and gender discrimination (Simon 2007).[3] In some respects, diversity has even become a dominant topic under the leadership of President Nicolas Sarkozy, who decided in the mid-2000s that promoting diversity would be central to his presidential service:

> I want to mobilize the entire state apparatus, the government and all ministries. I want the state to be exemplary. Exemplary in the implementation of policies in favor of equal opportunity, exemplary in fighting against discrimination, exemplary in promoting diversity, exemplary in terms of transparency on results. But the state shall not alone be exemplary. Exemplarity should also be shown at the local level. There are also political parties. There are also corporations.[4]

Along with the struggle against discrimination and the promotion of diversity, the notion of "visible minorities"—directly imported from Canada—is emerging rapidly as a key theme in French politics. Until recently, France was totally closed to such an idea, viewing it as pernicious and contradictory to the republican unitary tradition. Yet today, the vast majority of French public and private institutions claim that promoting visible minorities (Arabs, blacks, and Asians) will be one of their priorities for the years to come (Geisser 2007).

In this chapter we explore whether this conceptual and semantic revolution has actually changed the substance of political integration for postcolonial minorities in France. We argue that the changes in symbolic language have been significant but the underlying power dynamics remain the same. We call this new trend "nationalist multiculturalism" and claim that it is an adaptation of the French political elite to maintain power in a changing world.

Diversity and the New Ethics
of Ethnic Hierarchies in Politics

The success story of diversity in the French political arena is now in-
disputable. All political parties regularly nominate candidates who are
labeled "candidates of diversity" in all national and local elections.
Moreover, the concept of diversity now exercises an ideological con-
straint over political parties. All parties are now obliged to show, or at
least declare, that they promote diversity as a moral and political
imperative. However, we claim that this new focus on diversity has
perverse effects that actually perpetuate discrimination in four key
ways.

The Logic of Symbols:
Candidates and Exotic Elected Representatives

The first way in which this new diversity discourse promotes discrimination is political exoticism. Previous research has analyzed the ways in
which this dynamic was relevant for women in politics. For a long time,
women in French politics were relegated to menial tasks and given low-
status responsibilities with a patriarchal connotation (matters regarding
children, family, or health) (Achin and Lévêque 2006; Sineau 2001). In
many ways, France had undergone a superficial political feminization,
since the presence of elected women was purely symbolic and did not
consist of any real power sharing.[5]

Today, a similar symbolic logic applies to postcolonial citizens.
Often, minority candidates are used as visual evidence that parties have
complied with the new democratic creed, but in reality these parties have
only partially changed the distribution of responsibilities. These "elected
aliens" are mostly assigned to symbolic duties, and their presence has
more to do with public relations needs than with a real effort to bring
diversity to positions of power (Geisser and Soum 2008). For example,
after the municipal elections of 2008, there was only one mayor of
northern African origin in a country of over 36,000 municipalities. Most
elected officials of postcolonial immigrant origin have minimal responsibilities and only a small minority have become deputy mayors in
strategic areas (e.g., budget, economy, or public safety). We argue that
one way in which the focus on diversity promotes discrimination is by
highlighting minorities as exotic symbols that cannot access substantive
power.

Pragmatic Logic: Candidates and Elected Officials to Manage the "Ethnic Issues"

French sociologist Pierre Bourdieu has shown how the growing number of women in positions of political power has been accompanied by a division of labor according to gender roles. The highest-level jobs still go to men while positions of lesser importance go to women, supposedly to respect their "feminine nature" and their "domestic skills." Female politicians may appear to have the attributes of power but in reality are often locked into specific domains of competence (Bourdieu 2000: 136).

Similar dynamics exist for French citizens of immigrant origin. Their access to power is often based on an alleged "ethnic competence" for specific issues. For example, postcolonial elected officials are often assigned to positions in which they focus on urban problems, delinquency, or negotiations with the Muslim community. This means that the vast majority of minority political elites are confined to a subspace of ethnic politics and prevented from competing with the native political elite. In fact, contrary to popular belief, the ethnic diversification of French politics since the late 1980s has less to do with community mobilization and grassroots activities by ethnic groups and more to do with a division of political labor imposed by political parties to manage urban areas and Muslim integration (Geisser 1997; Moore 2002; Rinaudo 1999). This diversification has not fundamentally challenged the logic of ethnic segmentation in the French political arena. Instead, the diversity discourse helps perpetuate discrimination by channeling minority politicians into ghettoized inferior roles (Geisser and Soum 2008).

Market Logic: The Triumph of Ethnic Business in French Politics

The third way in which the new discourse promotes discrimination is by reducing politics to the rules of the economic market and treating minority communities as commodities to be purchased with superficial diversity (Blerald 1991). This logic has been especially promoted by Sarkozy's party, the neoliberal Union for a Popular Movement (Union pour un Mouvement Populaire, UMP). For the first time in parliamentary elections in 2007, the UMP fielded candidates whose ethnicity was meant to reflect the sociodemographics of their constituencies. This strategy was based on the idea that ethnic minorities have strong preferences for coethnic candidates, despite the fact that all serious French political studies suggest that voters rarely vote solely because of a candidate's ethnicity (Brouard and Tiberj 2011). For example, during the 2007 legislative elections, a UMP candidate in northern France of Maghrebi origin who was well regarded in his community (he is a professor of medicine and the former deputy mayor of a middle-sized city) was beaten in the second round because a large majority of Maghrebi voters preferred the left-wing candidate, even though he was not of northern African origin (Geisser and Soum 2008). Vote choice is complex, and factors such as political orientation, policy preferences, candidate notoriety, and social networks are often more important than ethnicity.

Although the results of this market strategy remain limited, French political parties have gradually internalized the concepts. In the future we expect parties to continue presenting more ethnic minority candidates in districts with large ethnic minority populations. The logic behind these strategies is similar to that of businesses that develop ethnic products (e.g., halal food products or Asian products) in neighborhoods where they identify concentrated populations of migrant origin. Admittedly, this dynamic might lead to more political influence for migrant-origin communities when leaders can leverage the threat of an ethnic vote. Yet, we argue that so far it has mainly perpetuated discrimination by using migrant-origin candidates as symbolic tokens valued only for their supposed ability to attract votes.

The Logic of Ethnic Lobbying

The fourth way in which the new diversity discourse promotes discrimination is by encouraging ethnic lobbying. Ethnic lobbying has traditionally been taboo in France because it is considered antithetical to the secular republican tradition (Lévy 2005). In the French political imagination, the concept of an ethnic lobby is associated with racism and the extreme right-wing anti-Semitism of the interwar years when ultranationalist thinkers denounced the "conspiracy" of Jewish elites (Birnbaum 1990). However, these taboos do not prevent French politicians from using ethnic lobbying when they feel it might be useful.

In recent years, French political elites have begun negotiating with leaders that claim to represent various migrant-origin communities. In the process, French political elites behave as if they were dealing with homogeneous groups (or tribes) whose interests can be represented by one individual. Often these migrant-origin leaders come from community organizations that were inspired by the prominent ethnic and racial minority lobbying organizations in the United States and are primarily focused on gaining access to institutional decision makers.[6] These are not popular movements mobilizing migrant-origin masses but elite negotiating networks that lobby on behalf of those masses, although it is not clear to what extent these leaders will truly represent the diverse interests of all postcolonial migrants.

To the extent that these new advocacy organizations gain prominence, it does not necessarily mean diversification and democratization of French politics but rather tribalization. Native-origin French voters can still choose from mainstream representatives while minority citizens will be limited to representation by ethnic particularistic candidates who are considered less universal (and therefore less noble) than mainstream representatives. Classic pluralist theories consider lobbying a way of insuring a vibrant civil society that promotes the interests of all citizens. In France, this new ethnic lobbying appears to be a mode of elite cooptation for the benefit of migrant-origin leaders that is disconnected from the political concerns of the masses of postcolonial citizens.

These four logics suggest that the rise of French-style ethnic diversity actually encourages new forms of discrimination and ethnic segmentation. This suggests that France has not broken with its old integration doctrine of blaming discrimination on the political immaturity of minority citizens. In addition, we claim that the new diversity discourse limits the capacity for mass migrant mobilization by fracturing migrant communities into new internal hierarchies. In the next section, we examine these hierarchies.

Diversity and the New Ethnic Hierarchy of Roles and Political Status

The discourse of diversity has changed the way in which the French political system relates to citizens of postcolonial origin, but it has not removed the divide between the "pure" native French and the French with "migrant origins" (Roman 2006). The latter category is considered less legitimate than the former, which includes politicians of European immigrant origin. In addition, the new discourse of diversity exploits several internal migrant divides: men versus women, black versus Arab, young versus old, and bourgeois versus working class. These divides evoke the classic colonial tactic of divide and conquer. In addition, they force migrant-origin elites into a postcolonial subspace of ethnic politics and implicitly forbid them to play in the field of legitimate politics (Bourdieu 2000; Geisser and Soum 2008).

The Issue of Gender:
Assimilated Women Versus Fundamentalist Men

Postcolonial women tend to receive better treatment than postcolonial men in French politics. Women are portrayed as emblematic figures of successful integration and the fight against patriarchal traditions from their country of origin (Geisser 2002). One of the most dramatic examples of this was in 2007 when Sarkozy chose three young women of West African and North African origin (Rama Yade, Rachida Dati, and Fadela Amara) as government ministers to symbolize the opening of the new presidential majority to diversity. His decision was based on the belief that the integration of minorities in the postcolonial French nation would happen primarily through women.

The June 2007 law on gender equality has greatly facilitated the feminization of French politics (Lépinard 2007). Co-opting women from postcolonial migration backgrounds onto lists of candidates allows political parties to kill two birds with one stone and meet the dual imperative of gender equality and ethnic diversity. In addition, focusing on gender diversity allows French political actors to behave as if men with postcolonial migrant backgrounds were less compatible with secular and republican values of French society and therefore less amenable to party discipline. As a result, minority men are excluded from political parties on the pretext that they are less attractive to voters at the polls.

The Question of Ethnicity:
Ebony (Black) Versus Beur (Arab)

In France, people of black African and Caribbean origin have long been characterized by invisibility.[7] The main reason for this invisibility is that blacks in France have not been considered a problematic population, whereas Arabs and Muslims have long inspired fear in the hearts of French natives. Yet, because blacks inspire less fear, they are rarely taken into account during the formulation of political strategies and partisan debates. Blacks have often been relegated to the neocolonial image of big harmless children who are useless in electoral politics (Ndiaye 2005).

It was not until the early 2000s that black issues became more present in French politics. This started with mobilization around the 150th anniversary of the abolition of French slavery in the late 1990s. In addition, Christiane Taubira (a black member of Parliament from French Guyana) sponsored a law in 2001 to declare French slavery a crime against humanity and then received significant support and publicity as a presidential candidate in 2002. Moreover, the creation of a new type of lobbying group, the Council of Black Organizations of France, has played an important role in denouncing the underrepresentation of blacks in the media and in political parties (Lozès 2007).

As a result, in recent years French parties have begun to support more French African and Caribbean political candidates but often by reducing the seats available for other minorities. In some local contexts, political parties have exploited the imaginary rivalry between blacks and Arabs as a way of confining them to an ethnic political subspace. This reinforces the trend toward ethnic segmentation and weakens the prospect for a common movement of ethnic minority politicians.

The Generational Issue: The Policy of "Eternal Youth"

Age is a third way of stratifying ethnic minority migrant communities. However, this does not mean that political parties juxtapose young migrant-origin candidates with older migrant-origin candidates. Instead, French parties assign all the political elites of North African, sub-Saharan African, and Caribbean origin to an eternal youth (Geisser and Soum 2008: 80–85; Roman 2006: 28). These activists, candidates, and elected officials are often referred to as young politicians, despite the fact that they may be middle-aged and have considerable political experience. This reinforces the stereotype of migrant-origin individuals as politically immature. In addition, it promotes the idea that these elite minorities are still learning about politics and must constantly prove themselves in order to deserve more responsibility (Memmi 1985; Fanon 2002).

This youth identity is also a social stigma. In the French public debate, "youth issues" are those of cities and working-class French suburbs, territories that are perceived as politically weak. For many French political leaders, the dominant image of Arabs and blacks is one of youth gangs who set fire to cars and contribute to social disorder. The way in which elites routinely refer to the youth of minority politicians perpetuates the idea that they belong to a class of politically uneducated people who must be trained before being allowed to enter the circles of power. One could argue that this training process might be relevant for young political activists of all backgrounds. Yet it is applied to post-colonial activists regardless of age and stigmatizes them as eternally young and eternally immature.

The Social Question:
The Ethnic Bourgeoisie Versus Hoodlums

In the 1980s, when the concept of republican integration still domi-nated the French political field, the civic association France Plus re-cruited electoral candidates of postcolonial immigrant backgrounds (mostly of North African origin). For the most part this process was elitist and focused only on professional North Africans (e.g., doctors, lawyers, professors, or entrepreneurs). The goal was to build a positive image of minority communities based on socioeconomically success-ful individuals. In addition, these individuals were supposed to be a new ethnic bourgeoisie that would take political responsibility for their communities.[8]

Similar tactics have been used in recent years. Although political parties praise the concept of ethnic diversity, they mainly seek a narrow slice of socioeconomically elite minorities. These elites are selected for their supposed capacity to separate themselves socially, culturally, and religiously from their homeland environment (Geisser 1997; Geisser and Soum 2008). They are generally members of the middle and upper classes, they are not very religious, they often preach a conformist dis-course regarding republican and secular values, and they generally live in upscale neighborhoods.

The main reason that these elites are considered successful is that they have broken with their communities of origin. They are valued for their capacity to produce an image opposed to that of stereotypical minority urban thugs. Yet, French political institutions also require that these postcolonial elites function as intermediaries between state institutions and their communities of origin in peripheral urban areas. This dynamic places the elites in a fragile and unstable position. When they maintain a sense of community with those who share their eth-nicity, they are vulnerable to being labeled narrow communitarians who are at odds with the French model of integration. On the other hand, if they successfully strip away all evidence of their ethnicity and become indistinguishable from other French elites, they will be disqualified politically and considered electorally useless.

Conclusion:
Promoting Diversity While Celebrating National Identity

The rising prominence of the concept of diversity has undoubtedly fostered a new awareness among parties and political elites about the urgency of fighting discrimination. In this respect, it appears that France is harmonizing with other European countries where the struggle against discrimination has been on the public policy agenda for many years. However, the French mode of addressing diversity and discrimination displays sharp limits. As we have argued in this chapter, the new diversity discourse also perpetuates new forms of discrimination and ethnic segmentation.

The new focus on diversity has coincided with a countermovement toward a renewed emphasis on conservative national identity. In this sense, France is unique among European countries because the leaders who promote diversity in politics (including President Sarkozy) also take chauvinist and xenophobic positions in the contemporary debate about French national identity. Instead of fully embracing a more open and inclusive conception of Frenchness, these politicians rely on distinctions between the "good French" and the "bad French," or between the "pure French" and the "French by adoption." The political parties also distinguish between "normal" elites and "diversity" elites, which renders the latter group illegitimate.

We call this new dynamic "nationalist multiculturalism." It promotes diversity in order to celebrate a Frenchness that is unique, universal, and supposedly superior to foreign models (Bertossi and Duyendak 2009). This notion may seem contradictory but it indicates the ambivalence of the French nation-state toward its cultural, ethnic, and religious minorities. The dynamic is partially inherited from classical French nationalism (Maurice Barrès, Charles Maurras, etc.), but it also incorporates the principles and values of postmodern multicultural societies. However, we should note that this ideological hybridization is not new. The Gaullist ideology at the founding of the Fifth Republic entertained "two conceptions of France, both contradictory and interrelated, gathered in the formula by which the French are assigned to play a central role in universalizing history because of the 'genius of their race'" (Colas 2004: 190).

Shortly after Sarkozy was elected in 2007, a government Ministry of Immigration, Integration, National Identity and Development Partnership was created. The novelty—which shocked many—was to include the subject of national identity among the major themes of government intervention. Throughout the subsequent national debate over French identity, President Sarkozy's discourse celebrated the myth of "eternal France" and "the richness of diversity."[9] This hybrid ideological development is what we call nationalist multiculturalism, and it is not a coincidence that the debate on cultural diversity in France emerged at the same time as the one imposed by Sarkozy on national identity. In fact, the simultaneity of the two debates reflects a deeper trend toward the importance of identity and the inability of opinion leaders to conceptualize the future of French society as it faces Europeanization and globalization. These issues are much larger than the contemporary fears of migration-related diversity and are likely to continue for the foreseeable future.

Notes

1. We focus on migrants from former African colonies and the French Caribbean because those from Asian colonies are not considered a problem in the French debates about migrant integration.

2. France applied the "Code de l'Indigénat" (the Indigenous Code) to the colonized populations (blacks, Arabs, and Berbers), which treated them as subjects of the French Empire and not as French citizens.

3. The particular language of this competition borrows from the business community debates about diversity, but it has gradually spread to reach all levels of the French political system.

4. Nicolas Sarkozy, speech at the Ecole Polytechnique, December 17, 2008.

5. Some might argue that things changed with the Parity Law (Law 2000-493 of June 6, 2000). This law requires political parties to have the same number of male and female candidates. However, parties often prefer to pay fines rather than actually build gender equality into their lists of candidates.

6. Examples include the Representative Council of Black Associations, the Council for Muslim Democrats, and the Coordination of the Berbers of France.

7. For more on this see, Fred Constant, "Les 'Noirs' de France sont-ils solubles dans la République? Notes provisoires sur 'l'invisibilité' d'une minorité visible" [Are black people assimilable in the French Republic? Provisory notes on the "invisibility" of a visible minority], report from the conference "Blacks in France: Anatomy of an Invisible Group," organized by the Circle of Action

for the Promotion of Diversity (CAPDIV) at the School for Advanced Studies in the Social Sciences (EHESS), Paris, February 19, 2005.

8. This group was also called the "beurgeoisie," according to a well-known play on words (Leveau and Wihtol de Wenden 2001).

9. Nicolas Sarkozy, speech on diversity given at the École Polytechnique, December 18, 2008.

5

Cautious Steps: Minority Representation in Germany

Karen Schönwälder

As of November 2009, Germany's federal government included a minister who could be described as a member of a visible minority. While his name, Philipp Rösler, suggests ethnic German roots—indeed the health minister was adopted by a German couple—it is clearly visible that he is the son of Vietnamese parents. Rösler's appointment could be seen as a political breakthrough, as a major step in the struggle of minority and immigrant politicians for access to positions of political power. If a German with Asian roots can become a government minister, why couldn't it be possible that a member of an ethnic minority group or someone with an immigrant background could become the leader of Germany's federal government?

Maybe it is indeed possible. Future election results and coalition arrangements are not fully predictable. Sometimes a political crisis leads to an exchange of personnel and the emergence of opportunities for newcomers. Furthermore, unless impermeable racist barriers exist, individual political careers of people with immigrant or minority background may occur while the immigrant and minority population as a whole remains largely excluded from positions of political power. The fact that a leading national newspaper recently presented Lale Akgün, a politician with Turkish roots, as a potential future federal president (FAZ 2009) illustrates that the election of an immigrant political leader has become conceivable.

And yet, it is easier to become a government minister than it is to become the leader of government, that is, a "German Obama." A leader of government needs the support of a significant share of the electorate, while a German federal minister is appointed by the chancellor and does not even have to have gained a seat in the federal parliament. Thus, the appointment of an Asian-German minister in the federal government demonstrates that in Germany the borders to political leadership have become permeable for someone of Asian background. Apparently, the political elite is prepared to accept such individuals in their midst, and they believe that such an appointment is acceptable to the German people. But to what extent is this shift the result of a broader advance of immigrants into political leadership positions? Does it express a general lowering of the barriers that prevent immigrant-origin communities from accessing political power?

This chapter assesses immigrant representation in German parliaments and local councils as of 2010. It is based on ongoing research conducted at the Max Planck Institute for the Study of Religious and Ethnic Diversity in Göttingen, Germany. As political leadership is of course not restricted to membership in parliaments, this is a selective analysis. Further research should include the full spectrum of political engagement, that is, in trade unions, nongovernmental organizations, and other aspects of civic life. At the same time, it may be that parliamentary representation is of particular importance to minorities as it symbolizes membership and acceptance in the immigrant society in a very prominent way.

Following this introduction, I provide some background information about the size and development of an immigrant electorate in Germany. In the next section, I discuss the relevance of residential concentration and the electoral system for the effects of the immigrant vote. Then I assess the potential for a minority representative holding the highest political office by analyzing the state of immigrant representation and variation across political parties, regions, and immigrant nationalities.

The Size and Development of an Immigrant Electorate

In Germany, people of an immigrant or ethnic minority background are commonly described as individuals "with a migration background."

This term includes residents with foreign citizenship, the naturalized, ethnic German immigrants, and the children of these groups. Beyond the foreign born, the second, and potentially even the third, generation are included. Statistics are based on sociodemographic criteria, not on subjective ethnicity. References to physical characteristics are unusual; neither the term "race" nor terms like "visible minority" or "nonwhite" are common. In fact, the overwhelming majority of Germany's immigrant population has European roots. Not even half a million have an African background and about 1.5 million had, or still have, the citizenship of an Asian country.[1] Asia in the German case mostly means Iran, Iraq, Afghanistan, or the Middle East.

There are 15.6 million residents with a migration background, which is 19 percent of Germany's total population. Of these residents with a migration background, 8.3 million (i.e., over half) are German citizens and all adult citizens are registered voters.[2] Citizens do not have to register in order to vote as voter registers are automatically drawn from the population registers. Estimates of the number of immigrant voters are based on microcensus figures. On the occasion of the last federal election (held in September 2009), the Federal Election Commissioner (2009) published an estimate of 5.6 million eligible voters with a migration background. This is close to 9 percent of the 62-million-person electorate.

This "immigrant electorate" is very heterogeneous, 2.39 million are naturalized former foreigners and at least 2.6 million are ethnic German immigrants.[3] A further 0.6 million were born as Germans of at least one German parent. Most of the naturalized former foreigners have either a guest worker or a refugee background. Those with former Turkish nationality are the largest single group among all naturalized foreigners, but they account for only about one-fifth of that group (all age groups) and less than 10 percent of the immigrant electorate.[4] At 1.15 million, those from Russia and Kazakhstan—mostly ethnic Germans—are far more numerous.

The development of a sizeable immigrant electorate has occurred mainly since the 1990s. The introduction of a liberalized citizenship law in 1999 accelerated the process. This law reduced the required period of residence from fifteen to eight years and granted certain groups of foreigners the right to be naturalized. Reforms in 1990 and in 1993 had already lowered the barriers. Before 1990, very few foreigners had become Germans. Of the naturalized former foreigners in Germany's largest regional state, North Rhine–Westphalia, close to 70,000 were naturalized before, but almost 570,000 since 1990 (MGFFI 2008: 101). And of the 538,000 former Turks recorded in the microcensus for Germany as a whole, only 39,000 were naturalized prior to 1990 (Statistisches Bundesamt 2007: table 7).

The 1990s were also a major period of ethnic German immigration, as the breakdown of the borders sealing off Eastern Europe enabled hundreds of thousands to move west. Since 1990, Germany has admitted about 2.5 million immigrants as ethnic Germans. Strictly speaking, a sizeable immigrant electorate of ethnic German background existed before, but was not perceived as such.[5] While the earlier Aussiedler (ethnic German return-migrants) often spoke German as their native language, those of the 1990s were a more distinguishable minority and more readily perceived as immigrants.

In the coming decades, the immigrant electorate that largely emerged in the 1990s will continue to grow. This will occur because of naturalization rates that are higher than those from previous decades and the fact that, since 2000, children of foreigners born in Germany (under certain conditions) automatically acquire German citizenship. By 2020, those of immigrant background may reach a share of around 12 percent of those entitled to vote.[6]

However, current low naturalization rates also indicate that a significant share of those with a migration background may not become German citizens. Out of an estimated four million foreigners who fulfill the residence requirements, every year only about 100,000 acquire German citizenship. Citizens of European Union (EU) states in particular, who account for about one-third of the foreign population, are largely uninterested in German citizenship (see Worbs 2008; Triadafilopoulos and Schönwälder 2011). Until the second generation, born as German citizens, reach the voting age, these other factors will limit the political power of the immigrant population.

The Force of the Immigrant Vote

In the United States and the United Kingdom, residential concentration has been a major, partly indispensable, basis of political representation. In fact, for members of some minority groups it seems difficult to gain a seat outside of districts with very high shares of minority voters (Clark, Putnam, and Fieldhouse 2010; Jones-Correa 2006). Apart from residential concentration itself, this situation is conditional on the existence of a majoritarian electoral system. Further, the ability to use residential concentration as a political strength requires that a group consciousness—based on (assumed) shared fate or shared ethnicity—exists that can be transformed into joint political action (see Lee 2008).

In Germany, the situation is different in all three crucial respects. Neither the electoral system, nor the settlement structures, nor the consciousness and mobilization of the immigrant population suggest that the driving forces of immigrant political representation could be similar. The electoral systems on the local, regional, and federal levels use forms of proportional representation. While there is variation, a pure first-past-the-post system does not exist. Nevertheless, constituencies do play a part. In federal elections, the overall number of seats for a party is determined by the proportion of votes for the party lists. But roughly one-half of the Bundestag is elected in the constituencies, and voter preferences thus influence *who* gets in.[7] On the local level, in particular, voters have been given increasing influence over the composition of the councils. Here they can, for instance, concentrate several votes on one candidate and change the ranking of individuals on a party list. It has so far not been investigated how such rules influence the opportunities for immigrant candidates.[8] In the regional state of Hamburg, where a new electoral system with multimember districts was recently introduced, there are indications that immigrant candidates could use it to their advantage. The Hamburg electoral system is, however, an exception in Germany.

To what extent are immigrant voters in a position to exploit the opportunities arising from concentrated strength in a particular region or locality? To what extent are they concentrated enough to represent a significant share of a constituency's population? Altogether, immigrant residential concentration in Germany is far lower not only than in the United States, but also than in the United Kingdom (for more details see Schönwälder and Söhn 2009). Germany's immigrant population lives almost exclusively in the part of the country that was the old Federal Republic, but is fairly widely distributed over that territory. This is equally true for the major national-origin groups. Of the Turkish population (here, Turkish nationals), only 7 percent live in Berlin, the city with the largest Turkish population. In Duisburg, the city with the largest share of Turks among its inhabitants, 12 percent of the population has a Turkish passport or background. This is not a very large share. And there are not many other cities where the share of those with Turkish background reaches even 10 percent.[9] Other large groups, like the Italians, the Greeks, and those from former Yugoslavia, are even less concentrated than the Turks. Only relatively small groups, like the Afghans and the Ghanaians, live relatively concentrated (with, in those two cases, about one-quarter of their nationals residing in Hamburg), but their numbers are too small to make them a factor in elections.[10]

Within cities, it is extremely rare that a district (Stadtteil) has more than 50 percent immigrants. Two examples of cities that have provided figures not only for foreign nationals but for all those with a migration background further illustrate the point: In Berlin, of 447 spatial units (Planungsräume), 36 had a majority of immigrants and their descendants.[11] The highest share was 68 percent (data for 2007, Bömermann, Rehkämper, and Rockmann 2008: 28). In Cologne, of 86 districts (Stadtteile), there were ten in which the immigrant share of the population exceeded 50 percent, and in four of them even 60 percent (data for 2007, Stadt Köln 2009). Typically, the immigrant populations are mixed and spatial subunits in cities where a single nationality group accounts for even 10 percent of the population are relatively rare, while in the United States and Canada shares of 30 or 40 percent are fairly common.[12] Thus, in terms of political mobilization, local strength seems dependent on immigrants mobilizing as immigrants rather than as an ethnic group. Furthermore, of those with a migration background, about half do not possess German citizenship and are not entitled to vote. In the Berlin district of Kreuzberg-Friedrichshain, 36.6 percent of the population has a migration background.[13] But the share of German citizens with a migration background is only 13.6 percent of the overall population, or 17.7 percent of the German nationals. In Berlin-Mitte, the district and constituency with the largest immigrant share, 16 percent of the population are German citizens with a migration background (Bömermann, Rehkämper, and Rockmann 2008).

In regional and in particular in local elections, constituencies are much smaller and it is thus more likely that they would have high shares of immigrant voters.[14] More studies will need to be done in the future to determine whether this has an impact on immigrant influence. A study in the large cities of the regional state of North Rhine–Westphalia provides some clues (Schönwälder and Kofri 2010). Here, those with a migration background, including EU citizens, account for between 7 and 26 percent of the electorate. In parts of the cities, their shares are significantly higher, but we do not have consistent data across all constituencies. In Dortmund, the state's second biggest city, immigrants and EU citizens account for 38 percent of the electorate in the inner city district (that forms four constituencies in the local elections) (Stadt Dortmund 2009: 32). In Cologne, although ten of the eighty-six Stadt- teile have an immigrant majority, due to the high shares of foreigners, probably no constituency has an electorate in which immigrants and EU citizens are in the majority.[15] This may also be the case for Ger- many as a whole. Due to the current settlement structures and low nat- uralization rates, it may well be that no constituency exists in which immigrants account for a majority of the electorate.

Still, residential concentration motivates the political parties to put up candidates of immigrant background, at least in some cases and pri- marily in local elections. In Cologne, three immigrant councilors were directly elected in 2009—all in constituencies with higher than aver- age immigrant shares in the population. In Dortmund, one councilor of Turkish background was elected in the district referred to above.

In federal elections, however, residential concentration rarely seems to lead to the nomination of immigrant candidates. In 2009, in Cologne's four constituencies, one direct candidate of migrant back- ground was nominated. Lale Akgün (who is of Turkish background) stood for the Social Democratic Party of Germany (SPD), but lost the constituency she had represented since 2005 and was placed too low on the party list to regain a seat. Remarkably, this particular Cologne constituency has relatively low shares of immigrant residents. The Social Democrats may have aimed at improving their overall image with immigrant voters by fielding a candidate with Turkish roots, but they do not seem to have targeted an immigrant vote in the constituency.

In all twelve Berlin constituencies, of the 60 direct candidates fielded by the five leading parties (Christian Democratic Union [CDU], SPD, Linke, Grüne, Free Democratic Party [FDP]) in 2009, only four had a migration background. Only one of them had a chance of win- ning, but here migration background was irrelevant as it was unknown.[16] In the heavily immigrant-populated Kreuzberg, the SPD- party leadership supported a nonimmigrant candidate who displaced the previous candidate, Ahmed Iyidirli, an immigrant with Turkish roots.

Of the twenty members of the Bundestag who have some kind of migration background, only two won direct seats. Most probably they won them in spite of, or regardless of, their migration background. There is no indication of any relevant immigrant mobilization in their support. At the same time, the election of Sebastian Edathy (SPD) and

Michaela Noll (CDU) may be taken as evidence that migration background, in this case an Indian and an Iranian respectively, does not necessarily alienate nonimmigrant voters.[17]

Of the three factors involved in possible immigrant electoral
success—electoral system, residential concentration, and group consciousness—the third is the one we know the least about. Do individuals with a migration background identify with other migrant-origin
politicians, or with those who share their specific national origin, or with
neither of them? Very little is known about this in Germany. In elections
to foreigners' advisory councils, national lists were often more successful than multinational formations. But the results of our own survey in North Rhine–Westphalia point in a different direction. Here we
asked prospective voters with a migration background whether, in the
coming local elections, they would prefer to vote for a candidate who
also had a migration background. More than 40 percent of the respondents said yes.[18]

The migrant mobilization that does exist has usually been aimed at
particular groups, typically those of Turkish background. Turkish-language newspapers often publish appeals to take part in the elections and
they introduce candidates of Turkish origin to their readers. After the
elections, they report the results for the Turkish-German candidates
(*Hürriyet* and *Sabah*, September 28 and 29, 2009). There are only
scant hints of a broader migrant group consciousness, for instance
when the Turkish newspaper *Hürriyet* (September 27, 2009) introduced the new government minister Rösler with the line that he would
be "the voice of the immigrants."

Altogether, conditions are unfavorable for immigrant parliamentarians to succeed on the basis of a mobilization of a regionally concentrated immigrant electorate. When immigrant candidates stand for
election, they have to win the support of an electorate that is primarily
nonimmigrant. Most of them enter parliaments via party lists. The
decisions within the political parties (i.e., of the party selectorate) are
thus of crucial importance. A list system and proportional representation are not necessarily disadvantageous for minorities. As Pippa Norris argues, in single member districts a local party organization will seek
to nominate a candidate who is likely to win the seat. For local party
organizations nominating just one candidate, there is no strong incen-
tive to contribute to an overall ticket of their party that represents the
diversity of the electorate (Norris 2006: 205). Immigrant candidates will
be nominated if their background counts in their favor—that is, if they

are thought to attract a relevant share of the votes of an immigrant or coethnic population—or if it is seen as irrelevant and they are nominated for other reasons. In some cases, a strong immigrant or ethnic minority party membership may push for representation. Proportional representation may have advantageous effects for the representation of disadvantaged groups if the parties want to present balanced lists representing the diversity of the population. The longer the list, the easier this is. So to what extent have German political parties been willing to put candidates of immigrant background on their lists, and to what extent have German voters been willing to support them?

Immigrant Representation in German Parliaments: Parties, Regions, and Parliamentarians

The presence of immigrants on candidate lists for German elections is a relatively new phenomenon. The first politicians representing postwar immigration entered Germany's federal parliament in 1994. Cem Özdemir and Leyla Onur were the first parliamentarians of Turkish background, elected for the Green Party and the Social Democrats, respectively.[19] Since 1994, four federal elections have taken place, and the number of parliamentarians with a migration background has risen to 20 after the election held in September 2009.[20] This represents about 3 percent of the available 622 seats, while almost 20 percent of the population and 8 to 9 percent of the electorate have a migration background. Of the 1,860 members of the sixteen regional parliaments, 53 had a migration background, which represents a share of 3 percent of the seats.[21] For the big cities, an analysis for the state of North Rhine–Westphalia finds 79 members of the local councils of 29 cities with more than 100,000 inhabitants, a share of 4 percent (Schönwälder and Kofri 2010).

Although still at a low level, the numbers of immigrant representatives have grown significantly over the past two decades. On the level of the states, Sevim Celebi in 1987 became the first member of a parliament, representing the Alternative Liste in Berlin. Slowly others followed, but in 2000, there were still only about a dozen regional parliamentarians of immigrant descent. The rise to fifty-three within the following years can be seen as a consequence of a new citizenship law (in force since 2000) that helped increase naturalization rates and signaled the political acceptance of postwar immigration.

The late development of immigrant representation is part of a history of anti-immigration policies. Since 1973, when guest-worker immigration was stopped, West German governments struggled to reverse its consequences. When the immigration of refugees grew rapidly after the 1980s, this did not lead to an acceptance of permanent immigration, but to frantic attempts to close the borders and to prevent the settlement of foreigners already in the country. The Conservatives, who led the national governments from 1982 to 1998, were committed to strengthening the German nation and the "German" character of the country. Only in the 1990s did the belief gain ground that at least a major part of the about seven million foreigners were there to stay and that their permanent exclusion from major rights could cause unacceptable tensions. Reforms of the citizenship law and the explicit acceptance of Germany's character as a country of immigration paved the way for an inclusion of immigrants in all political parties and for immigrant political careers in the mainstream. Yet, even if immigrant representation is growing, a closer look at some patterns reveals imbalances that should warn us not to expect an inevitable trend toward statistical representation.

First, the political parties contribute very unevenly to the growth of immigrant representation. So far, mainly the Green Party and, more recently, The Left have sent immigrants into parliaments and councils. Of the 53 regional parliamentarians, 17 belong to the Green Party and a further 13 to the socialist Left Party (57 percent).[22] Both parties together hold only 407 of the 1,860 seats (22 percent). In the previous decade, the imbalance was even more extreme when, for example, in 1995 five out of nine regional immigrant parliamentarians represented the Green Party. To an extent, the two largest parties are catching up. Even the Christian Democrats, the party of current chancellor Angela Merkel, now have 4 regional parliamentarians with an immigrant background. The Social Democrats have, in terms of the absolute number of seats, caught up with the Green Party, but it remains to be seen whether the larger parties in particular will be willing and able to attract a larger immigrant membership and open up paths to political leadership positions.[23] Given that, for instance, the conservative CDU has only 9 immigrant representatives among its 678 councilors in the twenty-nine large cities in Germany's most populous state North Rhine–Westphalia (Schönwälder and Kofri 2010), it still has a long way to go.

No party has yet developed an explicit policy to promote immigrant careers within the organization or to secure a number of places on candidate lists.[24] While they all state that it would be desirable to have immigrant candidates and representatives, their motivations for furthering immigrant careers differ. When the Green Party first put immigrants (who sometimes were not even German citizens) on candidate lists it was a symbolic demonstration of the party's multicultural identity and its protest against restrictionist migration policies (interview evidence; Villbrandt 1998). Additionally, because it was relatively new, its internal structures were more flexible, and open anti-immigrant attitudes were unacceptable among its members, the party provided a favorable context for ambitious young politicians of immigrant background. Tactical considerations (i.e., winning over immigrant voters) are only slowly becoming more relevant (interview evidence).[25] For The Left, a socialist party founded in 2007 as a merger of East and West German formations, it is equally true that the combination of new party structures where established claims to positions do not yet exist and a strong commitment to anti-racist ideas presents favorable conditions for immigrant careers.[26] In addition, the aim to attract immigrant voters seems to be a motive when the Left Party fields an astonishing number of immigrant candidates. Like the Greens, they do not seem to fear a loss of nonimmigrant voters in response.

Why the Social Democrats, traditionally the party many guestworker immigrants identified with, were slow to promote immigrant candidates is not easy to explain. In 1993, Hakki Keskin, a well-known spokesperson of Turkish organizations, was elected to Hamburg's Bürgerschaft as their first parliamentarian (above the city level). Others followed, but until 2000, fewer than ten Social Democrats with a migration background had been elected to one of the sixteen regional parliaments. In Berlin, as late as 2001, two women of Turkish background joined the SPD faction. In North Rhine–Westphalia, a traditional stronghold of the Social Democrats, in 2010 the first Turkish-German immigrants joined an SPD faction that, at times, has had more than 100 parliamentarians. As the SPD has long had many members with an immigrant background as well as links with social democratic organizations represented among immigrants, it should have a pool of potential candidates. The party is also likely to attract a significant share of the immigrant vote. In the absence of detailed studies, we can only assume that so far the relatively small size of the immigrant electorate, actual or assumed hostilities in the membership and among supporters, and established claims to positions of power and prestige have prevented a more determined move toward immigrant representation. But recently, at least in some regions and cities, the Social Democrats have begun to change their policy and implement policies that actively target immigrant voters. For example, articles and advertisements are being placed in the Turkish-language media and election leaflets are published in several languages.[27] Clearly the number of immigrant candidates, councilors, and parliamentarians is growing. After electoral defeats, in particular in the 2009 federal election, the Social Democrats have entered a phase of reorientation that could also involve more serious attempts to include the immigrant population. Indeed, the party leadership in 2010 expressed its willingness to make the SPD more colorful and more diverse.[28]

Likewise, the Conservatives seem to be worried about their continuing ability to present themselves as a Volkspartei (a catch-all or one-nation party). Both Conservatives and Social Democrats regard it as fundamental for their identity and the ability to dominate governments that they attract support from all strata of the population. While for decades immigrants were not seen as legitimate members of the German people, the leading political parties now increasingly perceive the immigrant population as an integral part of the German population and as potentially crucial for the ability to win majorities. Consequently, the federal leadership of the Conservatives has expressed the party's willingness to win more members with a migration background (CDU 2010). Its secretary-general has admitted that the Conservatives need to improve their parliamentary representation of immigrants and ethnic German return migrants. On the local level, in particular, the party was aiming to increase immigrant representation in its factions (Gröhe 2009). The party now has separate websites for "citizens of Turkish origin" and for the ethnic German return migrants.[29]

So far, the Conservatives do not have a significant immigrant membership, although this may be different for the ethnic German return migrants. For the latter, it is often assumed that they vote conservative, although the evidence is patchy.[30] It may be that the CDU and the Bavarian Christian Social Union (CSU) have so far taken the support of the Aussiedler for granted and regarded targeted efforts as unnecessary, while among other immigrants they did not expect to have much of a chance.[31] Indeed, both their Christian profile and a tradition of restrictionist migration policies are likely to alienate immigrant voters.

The liberal FDP is not known for any relevant immigrant membership and consequently has hardly any immigrant parliamentarians or councilors. But the 2009 election of Turkish-origin and Iranian-origin federal parliamentarians signals potential new developments. So there are signs of change, but so far immigrant representation is low and the political parties contribute very unevenly to it. Such unevenness can also be found in further respects.

Although immigrant representation has increased, on the state level it is still extremely concentrated in the three small city states of Berlin, Hamburg, and Bremen. Thirty-two of the fifty-three immigrant representatives have been elected there, that is, in states that account for only 5.8 million of Germany's 82 million inhabitants. This is not a reflection of an extreme concentration of the immigrant population: The share of Germans with a migration background among the population in the city-states is similar to that in the territorial states of Hessen and Baden-Württemberg.[32] For immigrant representation to increase significantly, it needs to spread to the large territorial states. Here the barriers are still very high. North Rhine–Westphalia before the 2010 election did not have a single immigrant parliamentarian; Baden-Württemberg, the next biggest state, in 2011 elected three. More research is needed to identify the specific reasons for this bleak picture. Access to political leadership positions seems to be difficult for all newcomers: In Baden-Württemberg, only 23 of the 139 regional parliamentarians were born outside of the state.[33]

Further, where competition for seats is higher, those of immigrant background seem to lose out. Whereas in Berlin there is one seat for about 16,000 potential voters, in North Rhine–Westphalia the relation is one to 78,000. Additionally, the immigrants themselves may be better organized and easier to mobilize in the city-states.

Such mobilization seems to occur mainly, if not exclusively, with the population of Turkish origin. More than half of the regional immigrant parliamentarians have a Turkish background. Other nationalities are represented by one or two parliamentarians.[34] Given that the share of the Turks within the immigrant electorate is estimated at less than 10 percent, this is a striking "overrepresentation." Among the immigrant members of the federal parliament the situation is different; here only five of twenty MPs have a Turkish background. The other guest-worker nationalities are only represented by a Social Democrat of Croatian and another with Spanish background. Four MPs have Iranian and three have Indian origins. The remaining have roots in Poland, Czechoslovakia, Ukraine, Denmark, and Belgium. But for the large cities—based on our sample of twenty-nine large cities in North Rhine–Westphalia—

we again found a dominating presence of Turkish Germans who account for almost two-thirds of the immigrant members of the city councils (Schönwälder and Kofri 2010).

On the one hand, this indicates that the immigrant population of Turkish descent is willing to participate politically and to adopt responsible positions. This contradicts strands in the public debate that assume a lack of integration effort or even a withdrawal into secluded ethnic communities among the Turks. Further, this is evidence that existing prejudices and racism have not prevented at least some local and regional party organizations from putting up Turkish candidates and have not prevented voters from electing them—although such barriers of course exist and constitute a likely barrier to higher representation. An equal representation of the immigrant population is unlikely to be achieved unless its political leaders are drawn from a wider spectrum of origins. The ethnic German immigrants in particular are hardly visible in Germany's political life. And of the large guest-worker nationalities, the Italians, the Greeks, and the Spanish have very few political representatives in German parliaments. Here, low naturalization rates are a factor that seriously limits political participation.

It needs to be further investigated to what extent immigrant candidates campaign on immigrant issues and specifically target immigrant voters. Members of the federal parliament who have a migration background rarely present themselves as representatives of the immigrant population. Only some parliamentarians have strong links with immigrant organizations (e.g., Sevim Dagdelen has links with Turkish organizations and Mehmet Kilic used to be a member of the Bundesausländerbeirat [Federal Immigrant Council]). The candidates of Turkish origin could rely on the support of ethnic media and used such media to appeal to potential voters.[35] But often they are also keen not to be seen as mainly a representative of their ethnic group.[36] Immigrant politicians in Germany almost universally state that they represent all voters in their constituencies—regardless of their ethnicity and origin (interview evidence).

Additional research is needed in order to establish how voters respond to immigrant candidates and to various migration backgrounds. Some recent research suggests that German voters are less likely to vote for candidates with Turkish or Muslim-sounding names (Street 2011). In our survey in North Rhine–Westphalia (see note 18), 74 percent of nonimmigrant voters declared that they would be prepared to vote for a candidate of foreign origin. In a Eurobarometer survey conducted in

2009, about one-quarter (26 percent) of the respondents in Germany said they would feel "comfortable" with having someone of a different ethnic origin from the majority of the population in the country's highest elected political position. Attitudes in Germany were less favorable to a minority leader than in the United Kingdom (50 percent "comfortable"), France (53 percent), or the Netherlands (38 percent) (European Commission 2009). While about one-quarter of the Germans state that ethnic background is irrelevant to them, the fact that almost two-thirds show reservations indicates that any aspiring political leader of immigrant background would be confronted with significant barriers. Indeed, among ministers and Staatssekretäre (state secretaries) on the federal and regional levels, individuals with a migration background are (almost) nonexistent.[37] Among mayors, a survey involving a random sample of 1,153 found 2 percent with a migration background, but none of them is a publicly known figure (Bertelsmann Stiftung 2008).

Conclusion

Given that Germany does not even have a well-known mayor of a big city with migrant origins, a "German Obama" is not on the horizon. And yet, immigrants are increasingly visible on the political stages of cities, the federal level, and regional states. A pool of aspiring politicians exists, and all political parties are now recognizing that they cannot afford to ignore the immigrant electorate. However, the level of immigrant representation is still low, and the imbalances between parties and regions should warn us not to assume an inevitable trend toward political equality. The mobilization of the immigrant population itself differs across nationalities, and the strength of the immigrant electorate is still limited. Altogether, Germany may well get another minister of minority background, but the example of other countries and of women's representation should caution us not to assume that political equality is easily achieved.

Notes

1. Published microcensus figures identify those with a current or past foreign citizenship. Figures are for 2007. Summary figures are given for Asia, Australia, and Oceania, but citizens of the latter two are not numerous. No

census has been held since 1987. The microcensus comprises 1 percent of all households.

2. Microcensus figures for 2008 (Statistisches Bundesamt 2010).

3. It is highly probable that a significant number of ethnic Germans are among those listed as naturalized foreigners in the microcensus. For example, this latter group includes 163,000 former Poles who were naturalized before 1990. But very few Poles—apart from those recognized as ethnic German—had had the opportunity to immigrate to Germany before 1980.

4. The Bundeswahlleiter (Federal Election Commission) gives a figure of 327,000 former Turks in the 5.6 million immigrant electorate. This seems a low estimate compared with naturalization figures in the past twenty years, but the discrepancy may be due to deaths and return migration.

5. How the earlier ethnic German immigrants were incorporated into political life remains underresearched, only the political behavior of the German expellees and refugees in the immediate postwar period has attracted significant attention.

6. This is my own very rough estimate based on the current figure minus an average death rate of 1 percent plus a growth rate based on current naturalizations and the number of immigrant children.

7. Voters have two votes, one for a party list and another one for a constituency candidate.

8. I shall use the term "immigrant candidates" to refer to individuals who immigrated to Germany or whose parents are immigrants. In Germany, *Einwanderer,* or immigrants, is not a derogatory term, rather it emphasizes that these people are here to stay.

9. We do not have comprehensive data on immigration background. In Köln, 8 percent of the population have a immigration background. Based on the share of Turkish citizens, we can estimate that in Heilbronn (7.5 percent) and Mannheim (6.4 percent) those of Turkish origin may account for about 10 percent of the population.

10. In 2008, about 50,000 Afghans were registered in Germany, of whom about 12,000 lived in Hamburg. For Ghanaians, the respective figures are about 20,000 and 5,000 (Statistisches Bundesamt 2010; Statistik Nord (www .statistik-nord.de/).

11. Such data exist only for a very small number of cities. Microcensus figures can only partly be broken down to the city level. Note that the definitions of "migration background" used by individual cities differ from that of the Statistisches Bundesamt (Bureau of Statistics) because of different data sources.

12. In a sample of 1,810 spatial units of big cities (units of about 8,000 inhabitants, cities with more than 100,000 inhabitants), in 9 percent of the units one non-German nationality accounted for more than 10 percent of the population. There was no unit where the share of one group of foreign citizens exceeded 40 percent of the population (Schönwälder and Söhn 2009).

13. The district roughly corresponds with the Bundestag constituency, which also includes a small part of an adjacent district.

14. In the Berlin constituencies for the federal election, the size of the electorate ranges between 183,000 and 232,000 (rounded figures). In local

elections, for example in Cologne in 2009, constituencies had about 13,000 to 21,000 potential voters.

15. Thus in one constituency in Cologne's north (no. 27) that combines three districts with extremely high immigrant shares, Germans with a migration background plus EU citizens account for 42 percent of the population (own calculation based on Stadt Köln 2009). The definition of migration background used here is not identical with that of the Statistisches Bundesamt. The city has not published figures for constituencies and voters.

16. Swen Schulz who stood for the SPD in Spandau has a Spanish mother; he lost the constituency but got into the Bundestag via the party list. Benedikt Lux stood in Steglitz Zehlendorf for the Green Party, Figen Izgin in Schöneberg-Tempelhof for the Left; the liberal FDP fielded Hanaa El-Hussein in Lichtenberg-Hohenschönhausen.

17. Noll's constituency, Mettmann I, is near Düsseldorf; 24 percent of the district's (Kreis) population have a migration background, but this includes foreigners. Edathy represents the fairly rural constituency of Nienburg-Schaumburg in the wider Hannover region. For another perspective on the potential vote penalty suffered by migrant-origin candidates in Germany see Street 2011.

18. The representative survey was conducted in August 2009 for the Max Planck Institute for the Study of Religious and Ethnic Diversity. It comprised 998 interviews in four cities, half of them with German citizens of immigrant background and EU citizens, half with nonimmigrant Germans.

19. Wüst and Heinz (2009: 204) additionally mention Angela Stachowa, who was born in Prague. I could not confirm whether she is the child of a Czech national. Stachowa was elected to the Bundestag in 1990 for the Party of Democratic Socialism/Left List (PDS/Linke Liste) and remained an MP until 1994. Some of the earlier MPs strictly speaking also have a migration background as they were born for example in Rumania (like Hans Raidel, MP 1990–1998 and 2002–2009, and Detlev von Larcher, MP 1990–2002) and moved to Germany in the context of World War II.

20. Own count on the basis of various sources; only personal information on the MP's websites, by themselves, or on the official parliament websites was taken as sufficient confirmation of their backgrounds. On historical developments, see, for example, Geiger and Spohn 2001.

21. The exact share is 2.85 percent; figures are for April 2011.

22. Figures refer to the situation in April 2011.

23. Membership figures for immigrants are largely unknown because German political parties have either no records or just figures for foreign nationals. The SPD, for instance, in 2004 recorded 2,794 Turkish, 710 Italian, and 573 Greek members in an overall membership of more than 500,000 (see Wiedemann 2006: 278).

24. The SPD in 2011 announced that it would introduce immigrant quotas for leadership positions.

25. According to the newspaper *Sabah* (August 20, 2009), Bilkay Öney, a regional parliamentarian, explained a growing support for the Greens among immigrants with reference to the Turkish background of party leader Cem Özdemir. Özdemir was quoted with a similar statement in *Hürriyet,* September 14, 2009.

26. This refers to West Germany, in particular. Here party structures are new and immigrants are put up as candidates. In the East, that is, the old German Democratic Republic, the situation is different, and the Left has no immigrant parliamentarians in its regional factions.

27. See labor minister Olaf Scholz in *Hürriyet,* September 2, 2009, listing reasons for an SPD vote, and the large SPD advertisement in *Hürriyet,* September 23, 2009.

28. "The SPD itself in terms of 'integration' requires a renewal. It is not diverse enough. The social reality of life is not reflected in our party, again, not only at the executive level" (SPD 2010).

29. See www.cdu.de/partei/15.htm. In Berlin and Hamburg, the party leadership has supported the careers of women of Turkish background. Emine Demirbüken-Wegner, apart from being a Berlin MP, is a member of the CDU's national leadership body. See also, for example, in *Hürriyet,* September 3, 2009, reports about a CDU conference with immigrant politicians where the general-secretary stated that, among other things, the CDU was a party of the immigrants.

30. See Wüst (2002, 2006) for survey results from 1999 and 2000–2001. In the postwar decades, the German refugees and expellees from eastern territories were a well-organized and electorally significant group. Toward the late 1960s, differences in the electoral behavior of those from past German territories and other West Germans disappeared (see Stöss 1984; Bösch 2001).

31. Or they may have relied on their established links with the organizations of German refugees and expellees of the 1940s. The two conservative parties, CDU and CSU, have the East and Central German Union, Union of Displaced and Refugees of the CDU/CSU, but the composition of its leadership suggests that this is a formation of people with pre-1945 links to eastern regions—not of more recent immigrants. The CDU also has a system of commissioners for ethnic Germans.

32. It is 12 to 13 percent in Bremen, Hamburg, Hessen, and Baden-Württemberg, while in Berlin it is about 10 percent (microcensus 2007, Statistisches Bundesamt 2007). Note: this is the share of German citizens, not of those with a migration background altogether.

33. Own count on the basis of the official biographies for the parliament elected in 2006.

34. Arguably, there are three parliamentarians of Yugoslav background. The example of Joachim Werner, a member of Bavaria's regional parliament, illustrates the complexities of German migration backgrounds. His father was a citizen of prewar Yugoslavia and, because of his ethnic German background, a soldier in the German army during World War II.

35. See, for example, Özdemir in *Sabah,* August 20, 2009; Kilic in *Hürriyet,* August 25 and 26, 2009; Özkan in *Sabah,* August 27, 2009.

36. Ethnic mobilization is a controversial issue among Turkish-Germans. Thus, the newspaper *Sabah,* September 21, 2009, published an appeal by writer Safer Zenocak not to vote for candidates just because of their Turkish background. In the same paper (September 24, 2009), Metin Hakverdi, an SPD candidate with Turkish background, criticized appeals to Turks to vote for Turkish-German candidates.

37. Rösler was the finance minister of the state of Niedersachsen before he joined the federal government. In this state, Aygul Özkan in 2010 became a minister for the conservative CDU. Tareq Al-Wazir, who has a Yemenite father and a German mother, leads the Green Party faction in the state of Hesse and would probably become a minister if his party joined the government.

6

Successful Political Integration: Paradoxes in the Netherlands

Laure Michon

Celebrated for its tolerance in the past, in recent years the Netherlands has become known for fierce public debates over the integration of immigrants and the place of Islam in Dutch society. Nonetheless, the Netherlands is one of the few countries in which non-Western immigrants have been fairly successful at becoming elected representatives.[1] In Parliament, foreign-born members have been present in significant numbers for twenty years. Similar success can be found at the local level. In the main cities, Amsterdam and Rotterdam, some non-Western immigrant groups are even overrepresented on local councils when compared to their share of the population.

Despite these successes, the number of non-Western immigrant politicians in the Netherlands is only one aspect of political integration. It is also important to understand how immigrant candidates get access to office and how their entire political careers develop. In addition to issues of descriptive representation (i.e., the physical presence of representatives who are typical of certain groups in society), it is important to examine the substantive representation of minorities' interests (Mansbridge 1999). This chapter assesses migrant political integration in the Netherlands by analyzing these multiple dynamics. First, I examine the levels of non-Western immigrant politicians in Dutch elected assemblies over time at the national and local levels. I then compare those electoral outcomes to the ability of non-Western politicians to make substantive contributions to Dutch politics. To further broaden the picture of political integration, I use a series of interviews conducted with councilors of non-Western origin elected in Amsterdam in the early 1990s and in 2006 to examine the factors that shape non-Western immigrants' access to the political process. This allows me to reflect on the difficulties non-Western immigrants face in developing long-term political careers. The conclusion provides an overall assessment of the positive and negative indicators of immigrant political integration. In particular, I claim that the number of non-Western immigrant politicians is a definite success, but their limited influence over substantive issues and their difficulty sustaining long-term careers point to significant integration challenges.

The Presence of Non-Western Immigrants in Dutch Politics

The Netherlands is one of the few countries in Europe where the percentage of non-Western immigrants in politics is comparable to the share of non-Western immigrants in the population. This is particularly true for the Dutch Second Chamber, in which 10 percent of the members of Parliament (MPs) currently have a non-Western immigrant background.[2]

The first "allochthonous" MPs in the Dutch parliament were Dutch citizens from the (former) colonies.[3] The first was an Indonesian-Dutch Communist MP elected in 1933 (Rath 1985: 53). The next, a Labour MP of Moluccan origin, was not elected until 1986 (see Table 6.1). Political representation for non-Western immigrants then increased more dramatically in the 1990s and 2000s. Eight MPs of non-Western origin or from one of the former colonies were elected between 1994 and 1998. By the end of 2010, seven of the eleven parties had at least one MP who belonged to a minority group, and seven different national backgrounds (apart from Dutch) were present in Parliament. For the most part, these non-Western immigrant MPs were elected to left-wing parties (and in particular to the social-democratic Labour Party, [Partij van de Arbeid, PvdA] and the Green Left Party [GroenLinks, GL]). Early non-Western immigrant MPs tended to be born abroad (or in a former colony), but in recent years they are more likely to be born in the Netherlands. Overall, the three main groups of non-Western immigrants in the Netherlands (Turkish, Moroccan, and Surinamese) are now represented

Table 6.1 Dutch MPs of Foreign Origin, According to Country of Origin and Party, 1986–2010

Term of Office	Turkey	Morocco	Suriname	Antilles[a]	Other (Moluccas, Cape Verde, Iran, Somalia, Afghanistan, Japan)	Number of Seats in Parliament
1986–1990					PvdA	1
1990–1994					PvdA	1
1994–1998		GL, PvdA, VVD	GL, PvdA	D66	PvdA	7
1998–2002	PvdA, CDA, VVD	GL, PvdA, VVD	GL, PvdA, VVD		GL, PdvA	11
2002–2003	PvdA, CDA (2)	SP, GL, PvdA, LPF	CDA (2), LPF		GL, LPF	12
2003–2006	GL, PvdA, D66, CDA (2), VVD	SP, GL, PvdA, VVD	PvdA, CDA (2),	PvdA	GL, VVD, LPF	17
2006–2010	SP, D66, CDA	GL (2), PvdA (2)	PvdA, CDA, VVD	PvdA, ChU	SP, PvdA, GL	15
Total seats in Parliament						150

Source: Data from Michon 2007.

Notes: a. The Antilles are part of the Dutch Kingdom, however, Antilleans are seen as non-Western "allochthones" in the official statistics (see cbs.nl). This table includes MPs who stepped down prematurely or entered Parliament during the term of office (especially during the period 2003–2006).

Abbreviations: SP: Socialist Party; GL: Green Party; PvdA: Labour Party; D66: Social Liberal Party; CDA: Christian Democratic Party; ChU: Small Christian Party; VVD: People's Party for Freedom and Democracy; and LPF: Liveable Rotterdam (Pim Fortuijn's party).

During the parliamentary session of 2003–2006, there were four MPs of Surinamese origin, two of them elected for the Christian Democratic Party, one of them for the Labour Party, and the fourth for the right-wing liberal party VVD. During that same session, there were three other Labour MPs of foreign origin, one of Turkish origin, one of Moroccan origin, and one who came from the Dutch Antilles.

in the Second Chamber at roughly the same percentage as their share of the population.

Non-Western immigrant MPs and their native Dutch colleagues have similar age and education profiles. All are relatively young (with an average age of 46) and they tend to have high levels of education. However, there are significant differences in the gender balance across the two populations. Among native Dutch-origin MPs, 43 percent are women while among non-Western immigrant MPs 73 percent are women. There are also differences in career trajectories. Half of all 150 MPs were elected to a local and/or a regional office before entering Parliament, but this was the case for only one-fifth of the non-Western immigrant MPs. Furthermore, while a large majority of all MPs (63 percent) held positions within the party or had so in the past, only four non-Western immigrant MPs had had responsibilities within their party. This suggests a difference in the recruitment of non-Western immigrant MPs, who entered Parliament with less political experience (in terms of party responsibilities and previous electoral mandates) than their autochthonous colleagues.

At the local level, the situation in the Netherlands can also be characterized by the significant presence of non-Western immigrant politicians and by a rapid and steady increase of their numbers over the past years (see Table 6.2). It is interesting to note that since 1985 foreigners have had the right to vote and to stand in elections at the local level in the Netherlands. This does not appear to have a direct impact on the presence of non-Western immigrant politicians in local councils when compared to the national level, as the number of locally elected councilors with a foreign background is not substantially higher than in the Dutch Parliament.[4] In some respects, non-Western immigrant representation among local politicians is even lower than at the national level (in most countries it is the reverse). The 303 councilors of foreign origin elected in 2010 represent 3 percent of the total number of councilors elected in Dutch cities, which is much less than the 10 percent of MPs. However, this conceals great differences across cities. In the main Dutch cities, non-Western immigrants are relatively well represented in local councils, while they have low levels of representation in the countryside (Dekker and Fattah 2006: 8).

Table 6.2 shows that there has been a rapid increase of the number of non-Western immigrant councilors in Dutch municipalities (it quadrupled in twelve years' time). In addition, there are important differences among ethnic groups. For example, the number of local coun-

Table 6.2 **Number of Councilors of Foreign Origin in the Netherlands, by Year of Election, 1994–2010**

Country of Origin	1994	1998	2002	2006	2010
Turkey	32	74	113	157	163
Morocco	7	21	26	66	66
Suriname	21	33	36	38	32
Dutch Antilles	1	8	5	6	7
Other	12	14	24	35	35
Total	73	150	204	302	303

Source: Dekker and Fattah 2006: 8; Dekker 2010: 7.

cilors of Turkish origin has grown faster than the number of councilors of any other group, while the number of councilors of Surinamese origin has remained stable over time. However, information on the country of origin conceals a range of ethnic origins, and later in the chapter I will argue that this variation is more significant than country of origin (Michon 2011: 91).

Among the non-Western immigrant local councilors, 35 percent are women, which is higher than the percentage of women councilors in Dutch cities (26 percent; Dekker and Fattah 2006: 9). The difference is less marked than at the national level, but again we see a clear trend toward the election of more women than men from immigrant groups.

The social-democratic PvdA has always been the party with the most non-Western immigrant politicians at the local level (more than 80 of the 302 elected in 2006), followed by the Christian Democratic Party (CDA) and the Green Left Party (Dekker and Fattah 2006: 9). Although many local parties compete in Dutch local elections and these parties gather a substantial amount of votes and seats (30 percent of all votes and the seats in Dutch local councils in 2002),[5] non-Western immigrants are rarely elected to these local parties (Dekker and Fattah 2006: 9–10).[6] Furthermore, parties based on migrant, ethnic, or religious identities are very marginal in the Netherlands and have rarely managed to win a seat in a Dutch municipality. It is mainly through mainstream national parties that the vast majority of non-Western immigrant politicians enter local politics.

Table 6.3 provides data on immigrant-origin councilors in Amsterdam, one of the Dutch cities where migrants have enjoyed the most

Table 6.3 Presence of Non-Western Immigrants in the Population and the Council for the Fourteen Districts of Amsterdam, 2008

City District	Share of Non-Western Immigrants in Population (in percent)	Number of Non-Western Immigrant Councilors in the District Council	Share of Non-Western Immigrant Councilors in the District Council (in percent)
Centrum	14	1	4
Westerpark	28	2	12
Oud-West	19	1	6
Zeeburg	39	4	19
Bos en Lommer	55	7	41
De Baarsjes	35	4	24
Amsterdam-Noord	36	4	14
Geuzenveld-Slotermeer	58	12	57
Osdorp	44	7	28
Slotervaart	43	10	48
Zuidoost	63	15	52
Oost-Watergraafsmeer	30	5	20
Oud-Zuid	17	2	7
Zuideramstel	15	1	4
Total Amsterdam districts	35	75	23

Source: Dienst Onderzoek en Statistiek 2008; data collected by the author.

electoral success. By 2008, 8 of the 45 councilors (18 percent) and 75 of the 322 district councilors (23 percent) belonged to a non-Western immigrant group.[7] The main non-Western immigrant groups (Turks, Moroccans, and Surinamese) are proportionately represented in comparison to their share of the population. Yet, there are interesting differences in representation among the districts. Generally speaking, the districts where the immigrant population is the largest (the western districts and the southeastern district) are those where the number of non-Western immigrant politicians in the council are the highest (up to 57 percent). Nevertheless, there is no one-to-one relationship between the two, as we can see from the figures for the districts of Slotervaart and Osdorp (in Table 6.3). These two districts have similar percentages of non-Western immigrants but very different percentages of non-Western-origin councilors.

To understand variation in migrant representation across districts, it is more important to consider district-level socioeconomic factors and internal party dynamics. Zuideramstel and Oud-Zuid, for example, are relatively wealthy districts in which the share of the non-Western immigrant population is limited. Furthermore, these districts elect candidates from either right-wing or local parties and these parties generally do not have many non-Western immigrant candidates. Internal party dynamics are important because local sections of the same party have different levels of openness to newcomers due to various historical dynamics. When those local sections are more open to newcomers, they are more likely to incorporate non-Western immigrants as members of the board or of various commissions, which then facilitates their election as councilors.

In Amsterdam, just like in other Dutch cities, there are ethnic differences among non-Western migrants in electoral success. Yet these differences are not as important as on the national level. Among the 322 district councilors, there were 21 councilors of Turkish origin, 19 of Moroccan origin, and 17 of Surinamese origin.[8] This indicates that Moroccans, Turks, and the Surinamese were equally represented on the municipal council after the 2006 elections. There were more non-Western immigrant women in the main municipal council (6 of the 8 non-Western immigrant councilors), and more men in the district councils (43 men and 32 women).

Two-thirds of the non-Western immigrant councilors in Amsterdam belong to the PvdA (7 in the council, 50 in the districts). This reflects the dominance of this party in all councils in Amsterdam. Other parties have only a few non-Western immigrant councilors. In addition, non-Western immigrant councilors tend to be affiliated with the traditional, mainstream national political parties.

These figures support the idea of successful political integration of immigrants in Dutch politics, both at the local and at the national level. Within a relatively short period of time, immigrants have gained access to the political elite and their numbers have risen steadily and rapidly. It took thirteen years from the 1985 enfranchisement of foreigners for non-Western immigrants to become proportionally represented according to their share in society (they became 8 percent of MPs in 1998). In comparison, it took women more than seventy years to become only one-third of the Second Chamber, and the political integration of the working class has also required decades of struggle (van den Berg 1983). All of this evidence suggests a positive interpretation of immigrant political integration in the Netherlands.

The Influence of Non-Western Immigrant Politicians

The descriptive representation of non-Western immigrants in the Netherlands appears successful, but in this section, I examine the extent of their substantive representation. Descriptive representation focuses on whether specific groups are present among elected bodies, which assumes that an elected assembly should resemble the population it represents (Mansbridge 1999: 3). In fact, Hannah Pitkin has argued that we could not characterize a government as being representative if it does not stand for the population and reflect its diversity (Pitkin 1972: 235). Moreover, when the whole population can recognize itself among the elected officials, political decisions are more likely to be viewed as legitimate (Mansbridge 1999: 12; Kymlicka 1995: 151). Some claim that another benefit of descriptive representation is its ability to enhance substantive representation. This is especially important for disadvantaged groups (e.g., non-Western immigrants in the Netherlands) because their presence among elected officials can include minority viewpoints that would otherwise be neglected (Mansbridge 1999: 12–15).

A full exploration of non-Western immigrants' influence on Dutch politics is beyond the scope of this chapter, but with the available evidence it is possible to say that the influence appears limited. One reason is that non-Western immigrant politicians may increase the ethnic, religious, and national-origin diversity of the Dutch political elite, but like native-Dutch-origin politicians, they tend to be highly educated and come from politically active families. In that respect, the homogeneity of the political elite remains stable.

Another reason to conclude that non-Western immigrant politicians have not developed significant political influence is that they have mainly joined traditional political parties and conformed to the status quo of Dutch politics. A few ethnic- or religious-based parties have emerged at the local level, and occasionally these parties have won a few seats. Yet these parties have primarily been very limited, both in scope and success. Furthermore, within the Dutch political parties, non-Western immigrants do not form pressure groups or other homogenous networks that could develop lobbying power. Ethnicity has not become a new cleavage within Dutch parties.

The growing number of non-Western immigrant politicians has also revealed the diversity of their ideological preferences. Although a large majority of minority politicians are members of the social-democratic PvdA (or other left-wing parties), there are many issues on which these politicians tend to disagree. A recent example was in the candidate selection process for one of the districts of Amsterdam. Two politicians of Moroccan origin (one who currently is district mayor and one who is a deputy mayor in another district) were competing for the first position on the list of the social-democratic PvdA.[9] In the harsh fight for this important position, one took a more polemical approach and embraced religion as a foundation for public policy while the other sought consensus among different local constituents and was more secular. Both candidates had similar origins but they pursued very different political agendas, which makes it difficult to collapse all co-ethnics under one unified political lobby (Michon and Vermeulen 2010; Schulte 2009).[10]

In many respects, non-Western politicians in the Netherlands have assimilated to the mainstream culture. They have not formed cohesive minority lobbies to push for the interest representation of their ethnic groups.[11] This helps explain why the successful inclusion of non-Western immigrants in representative bodies has coincided with a controversial debate on immigration, integration, and the presence of Islam within Dutch society. Non-Western immigrant politicians have been unable to prevent increased restrictions on the conditions for entry to the Netherlands, a reduction of the subsidies for ethnic and religious organizations, the rejection of the Dutch principle of *"emancipatie in eigen kring*" (emancipation in one's own community) when it comes to Islam, or more generally, the rise of a disrespectful tone in the public debate on how Muslims and Moroccans fit in Dutch society.[12] In fact, non-Western immigrant politicians have been fairly marginal to this debate.

On the other hand, one positive sign is that the current debate has not eroded the enfranchisement of foreigners. In 2007, the populist and Islam-bashing MP Geert Wilders questioned the legitimacy and loyalty of two secretaries of state, Ahmed Aboutaleb and Nebahat Albayrak, because of their dual citizenship. Later that same year, he asked for the resignation of an MP of Moroccan origin because of her activities in her country of birth. However, he and his party stood alone in these attacks and all other members of the Second Chamber refuted his arguments. In fact, ever since non-Western immigrant politicians got access to Dutch politics and foreigners were enfranchised at the local level, the idea that people with a foreign background or foreign citizenship are rightfully present in Dutch politics has never been questioned. Foreigners have become a full and legitimate part of the Dutch political elite.

In order to understand in more detail how non-Western immigrant politicians have gained access to the Dutch political arena, I now present data from a study conducted in Amsterdam over two decades. Using qualitative data on non-Western immigrants elected in the early 1990s and in 2006, I examine the extent to which these politicians have developed long-term careers and the nuances of their integration within the political elite.

Getting Access to Local Politics

In this section I examine the factors that shape immigrant political careers over time. My analysis is based on interviews with non-Western councilors in Amsterdam from 1990, 1994, and 2008 (Michon 2011: 75). The interviews from 1990 and 1994 were with twenty-three councilors of foreign origin who constituted almost the entire population of non-Western immigrant councilors in the capital city. They had been elected in 1986, in 1990, and/or in 1994 to the municipal council or to one of the district councils. The interviews from 2008 were with fifteen non-Western immigrant councilors who had been elected in 2006 (Michon 2011: 81). These data allow for an over-time comparison of how minorities access the local political arena. I use these data to pose two main questions: who gets access, and how?

The data provide a detailed sociodemographic profile of non-Western immigrant councilors. In the early 1990s, non-Western immigrant councilors formed a relatively homogenous group of young men (four women and nineteen men were interviewed) who were born abroad, migrated to the Netherlands as young adults, and pursued higher education in the Netherlands. Almost all had Dutch nationality. Their ethnic origins, however, varied considerably (ranging from Turkish, Kurdish, Syrian orthodox, Creole, Hindustani, Berber, and Arab), as did the socioeconomic status of their parents and the reasons for migration (some came to work, others to study, as political refugees, because of family reunification, or to join a partner who was already in the Netherlands). Only one respondent was a guest worker and four respondents were the children of guest workers, despite the fact that most non-Western immigrants are guest workers. The fact that almost all these councilors were highly educated men who were socialized in the country of origin is atypical for immigrants in the Netherlands.

The group of fifteen councilors interviewed in 2008 was very diverse in terms of age, gender, socioeconomic background, and history of migration.[13] In the 1990s, all respondents had been born abroad, but in 2008 four respondents were born in the Netherlands. For those born abroad, the reasons for migration varied greatly. Some came to the Netherlands for family reunification, others came to study or to seek asylum. Seven respondents were the children of traditional guest workers. The immigrants elected in 2006 were also different from their counterparts of the early 1990s because they had higher percentages of women and second-generation immigrants.

Despite all of this diversity, two factors were constant across all of the councilors from the early 1990s to 2008: they were all highly educated and all had Dutch citizenship. This supports existing literature on political elites, which identifies education as an important factor for political success (Lagroye, François, and Sawicki 2002: 468). In addition, the over-time comparison of the non-Western immigrant councilors shows that (almost) all have Dutch citizenship. This supports existing literature on the correlation between citizenship acquisition and political participation (Bevelander and Pendakur 2008). However, the idea behind enfranchising foreigners in the Netherlands in 1985 was that the political participation of foreigners would facilitate their integration in society even without citizenship (Jacobs 1998: 114). Yet the case of non-

Western immigrant politicians elected in Amsterdam does not support this line of reasoning as it suggests that naturalization is a powerful force for political integration above and beyond the right to vote, which suggests that foreigners are significantly disadvantaged despite their right to vote.

Generally speaking, non-Western immigrant politicians are not typical examples of their respective ethnic groups. Most of these politicians are far from the stereotypical image that many people have of non-Western immigrants (i.e., poorly educated guest workers with low-status jobs and underprivileged children). Some of these politicians arrived as elite individuals due to their family background and history of migration, while others gradually reached an elite position through higher education, civic activities, and professional positions. Most people intuitively link these politicians with an immigrant group because of the consonance of their name or the color of their skin, but they usually share more with their native-Dutch colleagues than with the mainstream immigrant population. In other words, their atypical elite status is an important advantage that makes it possible for them to access mainstream Dutch politics (Michon 2011: 91).

To examine more closely the details of how these non-Western immigrant politicians were elected, I turn to data on their political socialization and previous political experience. A large majority of the politicians elected in the early 1990s (seventeen of the twenty-three respondents) claim that their parents and relatives did not have significant political experience. In addition, most respondents started their political activities in the Netherlands and not long before they were elected: seventeen respondents joined their party in the three years prior to the election. For almost all of the candidates it was their first election and they had been asked to join the list, so it was not primarily their own initiative to stand in the election. Ethnicity was an important factor, as the following excerpt from an interview with a district councilor of Turkish origin reveals: "The board secretary of the party section here in the district wrote me a letter, saying that they needed . . . migrant candidates, and therefore they wanted to know if I was interested in standing in the election." Finally, most of the immigrant politicians had not held significant positions of responsibility within the party prior to their election. All of these dynamics suggest that the respondents can be characterized as relative newcomers to politics.

The explanation for how these newcomers were able to access elected office is the favorable context at the end of the 1980s and the beginning of the 1990s when parties were eager to have migrants on their lists. This was shortly after the enfranchisement of foreigners, and parties wanted to appeal to this new electorate by recruiting immigrant politicians. In an interview in 1990, one respondent described the eagerness of political parties to include immigrants on the lists in order to attract votes: "Up till now both the PvdA and the CDA and Groen-Links, and others, would go on their bended knees in order to try to catch immigrants. They won't always put people as high on the list as these persons would want, but they are quite useful." The respondents were not directly concerned by the enfranchisement of foreigners as they already held the Dutch nationality, but they appear to have indirectly benefited from this measure. Furthermore, in the specific context of Amsterdam, the district councils were created at the end of the 1980s and in 1990, which created an important number of new political positions to be held without any incumbents. In this particular context of little competition for positions, the inclusion of immigrants on the party lists was not very costly for the parties.

The electoral dynamics for respondents interviewed in 2008 were different in several respects. Nine (of the fifteen) respondents had parents who were politically active, mostly in the country of origin. In addition, the immigrant politicians themselves had been more active in politics themselves prior to being elected. Only half of the group (seven respondents) had joined a political party shortly before the election (three years or less), while other respondents had been members for as long as sixteen years and held important responsibilities within the party. Five of the fifteen respondents had stood in elections before and three of them had been elected before 2006. A large majority of the respondents insisted that it was their own initiative to stand in the election.

For many of the respondents, a transition period of learning about politics was necessary before they got elected. For some this took the form of working within the party, while others were active in civic organizations that allowed them to gain contact with politicians and learn how Dutch politics operates. This stage of learning about politics prior to being elected helped provide legitimacy when they did decide to run for office. One politician illustrates this dynamic:

> I had always been active within organisations, but I did not think about politics. I did not feel concerned . . . what should I do in politics? I was not trained for it. . . . But when I started attending the party meetings,

> I got stimulated. And because I was already active within organisa-
> tions, I thought that it in fact, it is the same, but here [in politics] I may
> get more things done.

Despite the fact that these politicians had diverse forms of political experience prior to being elected, the common theme was a background of
steady political and/or civic commitment.

The interviews with immigrant politicians indicate a change in
how non-Westerners access the local political arena. In the early 1990s,
there was a favorable context due to a new electorate and new political positions. This created a situation in which parties were eager to
include non-Western immigrants on the electoral lists. Fifteen years
later, non-Westerners needed more experience and knowledge of politics in order to get elected.

Non-Western Immigrant Politicians' Careers

The interview data examined in the previous section also provide valu-
able information on how the careers of non-Western politicians have
evolved. For the politicians interviewed in the 1990s, the average time
in office was seven and a half years, which is slightly less than two
terms. Three respondents stayed in office for twelve years. At the other
extreme, two respondents quit the council prematurely after three
years.[14] For the politicians interviewed in 2008, it is still too early to tell
how long their average careers will last. However, all eight of these
politicians were elected for the first time in 2006 and only three were
reelected in 2010.

On average, Amsterdam municipal councilors were in office for less
than five years during the period 1986–2002. Data for the length of
tenure are not available for all district councilors, but in the city district
of Slotervaart between 1990 and 2002 the average tenure was a little
more than six years.[15] In Dutch municipalities in general, councilors stay
in office for an average of eight and a half years (Tjalma-den Oudsten
2006: 5). These data suggest that the average time in office for non-
Western immigrants elected in the 1990s (seven and a half years) is similar to but shorter than that of councilors in general.

The majority of the respondents remained active in local politics
after leaving office. Most respondents held only one type of political
position, in the municipal council or in a district council, while a few

moved from district council to municipal council. In total, twenty-one of the twenty-three politicians interviewed in the early 1990s held political positions at the local level only. The other two respondents held positions in a regional council and one in Parliament.

Many of the politicians interviewed in the early 1990s were re-interviewed between 2006 and 2008 (sixteen of the twenty-three). This allowed us to address the issue of why they left politics. One of them explained that there is nothing specific for non-Western immigrant politicians when it comes to how long one stays in office:

> In the Netherlands, people stay in the council for a while, there is a hard core of people . . . let's say the die-hards who stay, and they make it a profession . . . but the large majority stays in office for a few years and then leaves. If I think of those who were in the council together with me . . . how many of them are still elected? Maybe . . . you can count them on the fingers of one hand.

It was normal for the respondents to quit politics after a few years in office, and most of them did not cite any negative feelings about the decision. They noted that it was the end of the term and they were not reelected, or there was a new job that was incompatible with their political function, or they moved to another district or another town (in this case, the seat is immediately lost). Most of the respondents stated that it was their own choice to quit politics. They usually thought it was time to do something else outside of politics, like returning to a full-time professional career. One of the respondents explained that stepping down did not mean that he disliked politics, but that he actually thought it would benefit his long-term political career:

> I wanted to broaden my horizon. . . . I wanted to do something completely different for a few years. . . . I had a job as consultant while I was elected in the council, but at some point I wanted to leave the council completely, I wanted to work in the private market sector for awhile.

I asked him why that was important for him.

> Because if you are totally immersed in politics, at some point you run the risk to become a bit dull, many things become self-evident, and you need to reset from time to time, at least that is what I think. . . . You need to reset your hard disk and . . . and try to do something completely different so as to get inspired and acquire new experiences.

In fact, even if the respondents no longer hold elected positions, most of them are still members of the party that they represented at the beginning of the 1990s. Furthermore, a majority of the respondents plan to return to politics in the future.

However, while personal ambitions are important, there is reason to suspect that non-Western immigrants face unique challenges in developing their political careers. A recent study conducted among ninety-seven non-Western immigrant politicians elected in Dutch local councils (Forum 2009) shows that while 77 percent of the respondents wish to have their mandate renewed after the 2010 elections, only 21 percent hold a secure seat on the party list. This study also showed that 75 percent of the surveyed non-Western immigrant councilors wish to pursue their career at another level of government. Given the data on the development of the careers of the non-Western immigrant councilors elected in the early 1990s in Amsterdam, the low rate of reelection among the immigrants interviewed in 2008 (three out of eight), and the data presented in the first section on the previous experience of current MPs, it seems unlikely that these ambitions will be achieved.

The careers of non-Western immigrant politicians in the Netherlands are relatively short and limited in scope. But to what extent does this constitute a problem? In some respects this is part of the broader picture of political careers in the Netherlands. There is a Dutch conception of one's political career as a temporary engagement followed by a more individualistic concern for one's professional career.[16] However, non-Western immigrant councilors have average tenures that are slightly shorter than those of the overall population. Given these trends, there is reason to believe that the ambitions of these recent non-Western immigrant councilors will not be realized in the Dutch political system.

I argue that if recent trends continue, they might constitute a problem for the integration of non-Western immigrants in Dutch politics. They could be evidence of a unique recruitment pattern for non-Western immigrant councilors, characterized by newcomers every four years who do not pursue their political career at other levels. To the extent that these politicians never have much influence, this could also give the impression that non-Western immigrant politicians are inexperienced and incompetent (for a similar mechanism among women, see Sineau 2001: 222–224). This suggests that success at accessing elected office is not sufficient for considering non-Western immigrants well integrated in general.

Conclusion

This chapter has revealed the paradoxes of the integration of non-Western immigrants in Dutch politics. Non-Western immigrants are well represented in elected assemblies in the Netherlands and they have been for many years. Furthermore, their access has been rapid and their presence is steadily growing over time. In addition, the legitimacy of their presence is not questioned. These are very encouraging developments that lead many people to believe that Dutch politics is very open to newcomers. But how can this be consistent with the polemical debate on immigration and integration in the Dutch public and political arena? And why have non-Western immigrant politicians not organized in order to take a stand in this debate?

Although non-Western immigrant politicians get access to politics without many obstacles, they do not develop long-term political careers. They hold a seat in a local council for a few years before leaving the political arena. This raises the question of whether the cost of entry is correlated to the stability and length of political careers?[17] Are immigrant politicians in Dutch politics the victims of the success of their political incorporation?

The data presented in this chapter show that the political integration of immigrants should be seen as a differentiated process, composed of different aspects that are not necessarily coherently linked to each other. The access to elected office may be fairly open, but this does not tell us how immigrants will be incorporated in politics over time, how their careers will evolve, and how the substantive representation of immigrants' interests can be assessed.

Finally, there are reasons to worry about the future of non-Western immigrants in Dutch politics. Some of the data point to the successful assimilation of non-Western immigrants into the Dutch political elite, in the sense that they are no different from their native Dutch colleagues in terms of educational and professional background. However, other elements suggest that non-Western immigrant politicians hold a subordinate position in Dutch politics. They have slightly higher turnover rates, minimal political experience prior to election, and limited ability to fulfill their political ambitions. When these factors are combined with the change in the public discourse on integration and the turn away from multicultural policies, it appears that there are clear challenges for the political integration of non-Western immigrants in Dutch politics.

Notes

1. With the term "non-Western immigrants," I refer to first- and second-generation immigrants of non-Western origin. I focus on these minority groups because they are at the heart of the discussion on integration in the Netherlands.

2. "Non-Western immigrant background" refers to immigrants born in a non-Western country or in a former Dutch colony as well as second-generation individuals whose parents who were born in a non-Western country or in a former Dutch colony. Persons who were born abroad and who have Dutch parents were not taken into account here.

3. By opposition to *autochtoon*, which literally means native-born, the Dutch term *allochtoon* refers to persons of foreign origin (whether born abroad or not), in particular of non-Western descent.

4. This lack of significant difference between the local and the national level with respect to the presence of ethnic minorities in elected assemblies may be explained by the fact that the enfranchisement of foreigners has little influence as a large majority of the inhabitants of foreign origin are of Dutch nationality (Dutch Statistical Bureau, http://statline.cbs.nl).

5. See Dutch Statistical Bureau, http://statline.cbs.nl.

6. Local parties are parties that exist and compete in elections only in a particular city. An example is the party led by Pim Fortuyn in Rotterdam in 2002, Leefbaar Rotterdam (which means: Liveable Rotterdam).

7. Prior to 2010, Amsterdam had one city council (with 45 seats), and fourteen district councils (with 322 seats in total). At the March 2010 elections, some districts merged and there are now seven district councils. Formally, the districts are commissions of the municipality and their competences depend on what the municipal council and executive delegate to them. District policies mainly concern the management of public space; the spatial and economic planning; and the welfare, culture, sports, and recreation in their districts (Barlow 2000: 277; Schaatsbergen 2006).

8. For one-third of the councilors (21 people), the names and photographs suggest that they are ethnic minorities, but the publicly available information (electoral material, newspaper articles, information on council websites) does not provide any detail on their specific origins.

9. The "lijsttrekker" (head of the list) of the party that wins the election becomes, in principle, the district mayor.

10. This obviously does not reflect all elements of the conflict between these two politicians. In the end, the latter of the two was nominated, won the elections, and is now the district mayor.

11. Michon and Vermeulen (2010) argue that important differences exist between groups of different origins in the extent to which they mobilize as a group. In particular, Turkish politicians and voters are much more likely to rally around their common origins than Moroccans.

12. Tillie (2008) talks in this respect of a hysterical debate that stems from the traumas of 9/11 and the murders of Pim Fortijn (in 2002) and Theo van Gogh (in 2004).

13. This group is representative of the whole group of non-Western immigrant councilors in Amsterdam on the basis of gender, ethnic origin, and party affiliation.

14. It was only possible to obtain this information for twenty-two of the initial twenty-three interviewees.

15. Slotervaart was not chosen for a particular reason, but the data was made available. Other city districts have not yet responded to my request for comparable data.

16. This belief is in contrast with the French conception of one's political career, which is based on the idea of a ladder of political positions, from local to national, and the accumulation of mandates. The ultimate aim is to become a full-time politician (Michon 2011: 110).

17. The data that I have gathered on non-Western immigrant and Antillean politicians in Paris and the Parisian region indicate that in a context of a higher cost of access to politics, careers are usually longer (Michon 2011: 111).

7

Race and Politics in the European Parliament

Terri E. Givens and Rhonda Evans Case

Although the European Parliament (EP) has not been known for having representatives of ethnic minority background, the body has played an important role in the development of policies related to antiracism and antidiscrimination policy.[1] These developments, which began in the 1980s, are an indicator of the role of the European Union (EU) in policy development. They also suggest that policies supporting the political integration of ethnic minority communities in Europe are not necessarily the result of bottom-up mobilization, but rather have developed from the top down.

In the 1980s and early 1990s, racist violence and the success of radical Right political parties across Europe catapulted the issues of immigration, xenophobia, fascism, and racism to the forefront. The European Parliament and the European Commission were instrumental in placing these issues on the supranational agenda. Although member states preferred intergovernmental cooperation and coordination of national policies against racist speech and violence, the European Parliament and transnational actors eventually supported a European directive that addressed racial discrimination in addition to racist speech and violence. This chapter provides an overview of the radical Right's resurgence, and through an analysis of supranational actions and member states' responses, it illustrates the divergent ways in which EU institutions, transnational human rights activists, and member states addressed the issues of racism at the EU level. As Europe moves toward closer integration, policy at the EU level plays a greater role in determining the initiatives that will be taken at the national level in regard to immigrant integration and race relations more generally. The political response to racism was clearly an important factor placing these issues on the agenda and in the development of policy at the EU level, which is now in the process of being implemented by member states.

A Resurgent Radical Right

At the EP's 1984 elections, sixteen members of radical Right political parties were elected to sit in Strasbourg. France's Front National (FN) sent ten members, including Jean-Marie Le Pen; the remainder belonged to Italy's neofascist Movimento Sociale Italiano (Italian Social Movement, MSI), which had increased its representation from four in 1979 to five, and Greece's Ethniki Politiki Enossis (National Civil Union), which returned its single member. As a result of this performance, the radical Right was able to establish the Group of the European Right in the EP, thereby gaining substantial financial support and political legitimacy. In 1989, Germany's Republikaner Party won 7.1 percent of the vote in elections for the EP, while the FN increased its vote slightly from 11.2 percent in 1984 to 11.7 percent in 1989 (Givens 2005). At this point, Britain's first-past-the-post electoral system effectively ruled out seats for any extreme parties.[2]

The FN also fared well in French elections for domestic office. The party won 9.7 percent of the vote in France's national parliamentary elections in 1986, and a temporary switch to proportional representation led to the party winning thirty-five seats in the French Assembly. The rules were returned to first past the post in the 1988 election, and the FN was unable to win any seats despite receiving 9.7 percent of the vote again. At the 1993 election, the FN improved to 12.4 percent of the vote; however, they did not win any seats. Le Pen received 14.4 percent of the vote in the first round of the 1988 French presidential election, but did not make it into the second round (Givens 2005).

In Germany, the Republikaner and the German People's Union (DVU) performed well in a series of state and local elections during the 1980s and early 1990s. Historically, the National Democratic Party

(NPD) had been the main party on the extreme right in Germany, winning as much as 4.3 percent of the vote in the 1969 Bundestag elections. The Republikaner, established in 1983, was initially led by a former Waffen-SS officer, and campaigned on a "strong antiforeigner theme" (Conradt 2005: 113). At the 1989 West Berlin election, the Republikaner campaigned heavily on the issue of immigration and took 7.5 percent of the vote (Givens 2005). Three years later and after the fall of the Berlin Wall, the Republikaner won 10.9 percent of the vote in the state of Baden-Württemburg, winning a block of seats and a foothold in an important state. The Christian Democratic Union (CDU) was particularly affected by the Republikaner's success, losing voters at twice the rate of the Social Democratic Party (SPD). The DVU was formed in 1987 in Bavaria and had some minor success at the state level. The party eventually joined with the NPD for state elections in the former East Germany, having minor success at the regional level.

France and Germany were not the only countries to experience a resurgent radical Right. Austria's Freedom Party (FPÖ) saw consistent gains after Jörg Haider took over control of the party in 1986. It began to challenge the mainstream parties during the 1990s, culminating in the party winning over 27 percent of the vote in the 1999 legislative election and joining a coalition with the conservative People's Party. Although the FPÖ was only able to contest European Parliament elections after 1995, the year in which Austria abandoned its post–World War II neutrality and joined the EU, the FPÖ's success still influenced Europe's deliberations over xenophobia and racism (Givens 2005). In Denmark, the People's Party gained enough seats in Parliament to support the minority government and have a major impact in legislation related to immigrants.

Europe Responds

EU institutions and member states responded to the foregoing developments in different ways. Four months after the 1984 EP elections, the European Parliament established a Committee of Inquiry to examine the "Rise of Fascism and Racism in Europe." This committee, which became known as the "Evrigenis Committee" after its rapporteur, Dimitrios Evrigenis, was ultimately created over the objections of Le Pen, by then a member of the European Parliament (MEP) (Evrigenis Committee, "Report of the Committee of Inquiry into the Rise of Fascism and Racism in Europe" [hereinafter Evrigenis Report] 1985: 10–11). The EP charged the committee with examining links between anti-immigrant groups and the potential causes of their proliferation as well as the policies employed by member states for combating these types of organizations (Evrigenis Report 1985: 11). The Evrigenis Committee's report pays relatively little attention to the phenomenon of racial discrimination and to national antidiscrimination laws as opposed to laws that target racist speech and hate crimes (Evrigenis Report 1985: 82–84).

Despite its limited definition of the problem, among its forty-one recommendations, the committee encouraged member states to adopt several policies that related to discrimination. These included establishing "effective means of legal recourse in disputes relating to racial discrimination" and guaranteeing nongovernmental organizations (NGOs) a "right to institute civil proceedings." It also recommended that the EU's powers and responsibilities in the area of "race relations" be defined "more broadly." This, the Evrigenis Committee suggested, could be accomplished in any of three ways: first, through a liberal interpretation of the existing treaty provisions and the EU's implicit powers; second, pursuant to Article 235 of the Treaty Establishing the European Community (TEEC, also known as the Treaty of Rome), which allows for an expansion of European authority, with the European Council's unanimous support, in order to achieve an EU objective; or third, "if necessary," through a revision of the TEEC (Evrigenis Report 1985: 95–96, 104–105).[3]

In 1986, the council realized one of the Evrigenis Report's recommendations by joining the EP and European Commission in formally condemning racism and xenophobia by means of a joint declaration.[4] This measure also defined the problem narrowly, focusing on the "growth of xenophobic attitudes, movements and acts of violence" that are "often directed against immigrants" (reprinted in European Commission 1997: 12).[5] However, in contrast to the Evrigenis Committee, the declaration virtually ignored the issue of discrimination— only its final sentence acknowledges a "need to ensure that all acts or forms of discrimination are prevented or curbed." Moreover, endorsing purely intergovernmental solutions, it neither committed member states to specific, domestic policy actions nor set forth a basis for the development of EU competency in this policy area. As the council's first formal recognition of the problem of racism, this joint declaration is symbolically important. In substantive terms, however, it has been described as "a simple insipid document" that constitutes nothing more than a "false dawn in policy on racial discrimination" (German MEP Franz-Ludwig Schenk Graf von Stauffenberg, quoted in Bleich and Feldmann 2004: fn. 3).

The European Commission and the EP nevertheless continued to press member states for more meaningful action on the issues of racism and discrimination. In 1988, the commission submitted a proposal to the council for a resolution on racism and xenophobia that would have encouraged member states to adopt antidiscrimination legislation where it did not already exist and enhance the effectiveness of existing legislation by revising definitions of discrimination and improving access to justice. Its proposal echoed policy recommendations that had appeared in the Evrigenis Report. Although the resolution was to be nonbinding, it still took two years for the council to reach agreement on a considerably weaker version of the commission's initial proposal. As these negotiations dragged on, the EP convened a new Committee of Inquiry, with Glyn Ford (MEP) as rapporteur, to produce a second report on racism and xenophobia. The council ultimately adopted a resolution in 1990 that acknowledged that "acts inspired by racism and xenophobia may be countered by legislative or institutional measures," including antidiscrimination laws, authorizing NGOs the right to initiate or support legal proceedings, and the provision of legal assistance.[6] However, it did not obligate member states to take any of these actions, nor did it express support for granting the EU competency in this policy area. In fact, the council annexed a declaration to the resolution expressly providing that its implementation may *not* lead to an enlargement of the EU's competency as defined by the Treaty of Rome (Ford 1992: 101). The following year, the EP released the "Ford Report." Among its seventy-seven proposals, most of which focused on immigrants and third country nationals (TCNs), it recommended that member states enact antidiscrimination laws "condemning all racist acts" and enabling "associations to bring prosecutions for racist acts or appear as joint plaintiffs" (Ford 1992: 159–160).

The production of the Evrigenis and Ford reports were critical first steps in the recognition of issues related to immigration, racism, and discrimination at the EU level. Although they did not lead to immediate legislation on the part of the commission, they were the building blocks that would lead other actors to step in and take action on these issues.

A Transnational Actor Emerges:
The Starting Line Group

A variety of organizations had been lobbying on behalf of immigrants and racial and ethnic minorities in the 1980s. By 1992, activists realized that the EU was being used to construct "Fortress Europe." This experience catalyzed them to look for other, more propitious means of advancing their interests in order to ameliorate the effects of restrictive immigration, asylum, and citizenship policies (Dummett 1991; Bell 2002: 68). Activists, therefore, reframed the problem as one of racism and discrimination (Chalmers 2000). Having redefined the problem, a new set of solutions concomitantly followed. The enactment of antidiscrimination laws, predominantly at the EU level, became a priority, particularly after a group of activists and NGOs mobilized around this policy solution.

In 1991, a variety of activists and NGOs coalesced into a loose transnational advocacy network that would call itself the "Starting Line Group" (SLG). The idea for such a network was conceived at a meeting of lawyers, activists, and experts, including government advisers, a former member of the European Commission, and civil servants from six countries (Belgium, France, Germany, Italy, the Netherlands, and the UK). From the beginning, several organizations assumed a leading role, including the Churches' Committee for Migrants in Europe (CCME), a transnational NGO, as well as Britain's Commission on Racial Equality and the Dutch National Bureau against Racism, two quasi-state organizations that had been created for purposes of addressing issues concerning immigrants and racial or ethnic minorities at the national level. They were subsequently joined by Belgium's Royal Commission on Policy Towards Immigrants. Eventually, Jan Niessen, the secretary general of the CCME, would form the Migration Policy Group (MPG), a Brussels-based think tank that after 1996 would serve as the group's coordinating body (Niessen 2000b: 502).

The organizers decided to draft an antidiscrimination directive and develop a lobbying campaign around it (Dummett 1994: 530; Chopin 1999b: 111; Chopin and Niessen 2001). They accepted, as had been suggested in the Evrigenis Report (1985), that the EU possessed the requisite authority under the existing treaty provisions to adopt such a measure.[7] By 1992, the group had produced its proposal, "The Starting Line," from which the loose coalition of organizations took its name. This proposed directive was translated into all of the languages of the twelve member states and disseminated widely (Niessen 2000b: 501). In addition, in 1994, a copy of "The Starting Line" was reproduced in the publication *New Community* (see Dummett 1994).

Prior to the SLG's establishment, there was "very little coordination of national and EU-level actors" working on behalf of immigrants and against racism (Wallace 2000: 192). Various groups and activists appeared before the EP's Evrigenis and Ford committees, and two in particular, the Brussels-based Migration News Sheet, which collected country-by-country information on racial discrimination, and the London-based Searchlight, which collected information on extremist right-wing organizations, assisted the Ford Committee in the production of its 1992 report (Niessen 2000b: 494). Nevertheless, collective action was inhibited because most pro-immigrant organizations saw the EU as a forum in which immigrant interests were more likely to be undermined than advanced (Niessen 2000b). In addition, although a variety of antiracism organizations existed across Europe, they experienced difficulty in focusing their effort and coordinating their activities (Ruzza 2000). The multiplicity of issues and policy priorities inhibited effective collective action.

The SLG surmounted these obstacles by devising a campaign that had a single focus—the adoption of an EU directive against racial discrimination (Chopin 1999b: 111). According to Jan Niessen of the MPG, "We never wanted to be bothered by anything else—petitions, conferences—we focused only on legislation" (Freedom House 2005; see also Dummett 1994: 530; Chopin 1999a: 2). By various reports, the coalition's membership eventually grew to include several hundred organizations, such as the Struggle Against Racism, the Commissioner for Foreigners' Affairs of the Senate of Berlin, Caritas Europe, the European Jewish Information Network, the Migrants Forum, the European Anti-Poverty Network, and the European Roma Rights Centre, among others (see Dummett 1994: fn. 1; Chopin 1999b: 111; Niessen 2000b: 496). The MPG coordinated the network's efforts, and by design, it rarely sought to convene the SLG as a group. According to Niessen, it was thought that members of the group should "never" be brought together precisely because of their varied and potentially conflicting interests (Freedom House 2005). If the SLG were convened, the leadership feared that talk of other issues would potentially weaken the coalition.

The SLG's single-minded focus on a directive also facilitated the practice of "accountability politics" (Keck and Sikkink 1998). The council had expressly acknowledged the problems of racism and discrimination and endorsed the need for their eradication. By offering member states a specific, targeted policy solution, rather than an assemblage of myriad policies, as had previous EP reports, the SLG could pressure member states to take action. The SLG formally launched its Starting Line proposal in the lead-up to the European Council's 1992 Edinburgh Summit. Thereafter, references to the problem of racism regularly appeared in the Presidency Conclusions that were published after each meeting of the European Council between 1992 and 1997, but member states refrained from taking further action on the basis that the EU did not possess authority to adopt racial antidiscrimination policy under the current treaty provisions.

In addition, the SLG forged important relationships with both the EP and the Commission. Parliament endorsed the SLG's draft directive in two resolutions and explicitly asked the Commission to use the Starting Line proposal as a basis for drawing up a directive aimed at harmonizing legal measures in the member states to eliminate racial discrimination.[8] These actions kept the proposal on the agenda and enhanced the credibility of the proposal as well as that of the SLG as a key player in this policy area. The Commission, by contrast, withheld formal expressions of support for the Starting Line and refrained from using its power to submit to the council a proposal for such a directive. Commissioners were divided on the issue of the EU's legal authority to adopt such a directive absent a treaty amendment. In addition, based upon the Commission's experience with the 1990 Resolution, they feared that member states would weaken or reject any such proposal and thereby make the Commission look weak (Chopin and Niessen 2001: 101).

Realizing that insufficient political will existed within the Commission and among member states to rely on existing treaty authority as the basis for a directive, in 1993 the SLG shifted its strategy to seeking an amendment to the Treaty on European Union (TEU) that would expressly provide the EU with authority to adopt an antidiscrimination directive on grounds other than gender (Chopin 1999b: 115; Bell 2002: 63; Dummett 1994: 530). This tactical adjustment proved consequential. Member states were on record denouncing racism since the 1986 Joint Resolution, yet the claim of insufficient treaty authority provided a convenient excuse for inaction at the EU level (Wallace 2000). Securing a treaty amendment would require the unanimous consent of member states, a particularly difficult proposition, especially while the Conservatives continued to govern Britain. Yet, just four years after the SLG released its Starting Point proposal, Article 13 was adopted. What happened during this period to produce such an unexpected result?

The Development of Article 13

At its 1994 meeting in the Greek city of Corfu, the European Council acted on a proposal by French president François Mitterrand and German chancellor Helmut Kohl and established the "Kahn Commission." This Commission ultimately recommended that the treaty be amended to assign the EU competency over racial antidiscrimination policy, and it played a key role in setting the agenda for the 1996–1997 Intergovernmental Conference (IGC) at which Article 13 was adopted. Although the French and German politicians may have been acting on the basis of short-term political concerns related to the rise of radical Right parties, the Kahn Commission's report led to major new developments in the pursuit of antidiscrimination legislation at the EU level. In creating the Kahn Commission, scholars suggest French and German preferences were transformed by perceived threats from the radical Right (Wallace 2000: 153–197). The success of right-wing parties prompted responses from mainstream parties at the national level.

During the early 1990s, right-wing extremism was on the rise in Germany. Following an improved showing in the March 1993 state election in Hesse, fears were expressed in the popular media that the Republikaner could surmount the 5 percent threshold at the following year's election and thereby gain seats in the Bundestag (Doyle 1993). The prospect of the Republikaner holding the balance of power led the CDU to declare that it would not enter into coalition with any group that threatened democracy (Givens 2005). In the early 1990s, Germany experienced an escalation in racist violence against ethnic minorities and modest growth in neo-Nazi groups (Givens 2005). For example, 17 people were killed and 2,500 were injured in a surge of racist violence in 1992 (Doyle 1993). In May 1994, Kohl met leaders of Jewish organizations, including Jean Kahn, as part of an ongoing round of talks on racist violence. His government introduced a bill that would strengthen Germany's criminal law against incitement to racial hatred in December 1994.[9]

In March 1993, the Right swept into power in the French National Assembly, inaugurating a period of cohabitation with Prime Minister

Edouard Balladur and the appointment of Charles Pasqua, a hardliner on immigration, as interior minister. Pasqua implemented many of the FN's immigration and citizenship proposals, rejecting only the most extreme (Simmons 1996: 106). Meanwhile, popular approval of the FN had declined. In one poll, 79 percent of respondents said they disagreed with the Front, and 73 percent agreed that Le Pen and the Front posed a danger to democracy, although 61 percent agreed with Le Pen's stance on immigration (Simmons 1996: 103, 105). In pushing for the Kahn Commission, Mitterrand probably sought to counterbalance the Balladur government. His support risked little political cost because France already had antiracism policies in place, and public opinion polls indicated French discomfort with the hard edge of the FN's racist appeals. Mitterrand could thus safely assume that French voters would not punish him for a supranational effort against racist speech and violence.

The Kahn Commission issued several interim reports between November 1994 and its final report in 1996 in which it recommended amending the Maastricht Treaty (TEU) in order to give the EU competency to enact policy against racial discrimination. During this period, the Euro-skeptical Conservatives remained in power in Britain, thus providing a constant source of resistance, but national governments more generally showed little interest in the Kahn Commission's recommendation, according to public accounts by SLG activists (Niessen 2000a: 496; Chopin and Niessen 2001: 99, fn. 18).

A review of the Presidency Conclusions that were published after each meeting of the European Council between 1994 and 1996 reinforces this assessment. These conclusions summarize the main issues discussed at the meetings and thus serve as an accurate barometer of member-state concerns, particularly those of the governments that held the presidency of the council and thus chaired the meetings. They reveal a pattern by which the council regularly acknowledged the problem of racism but issued symbolic gestures rather than substantive policy commitments. Even the June 1995 European Council in Cannes did not engage the interim report that had been issued by the Kahn Commission just two months earlier and in which the Commission proposed an amendment to the TEU (Wallace 2000: 122, 163–166). Instead, it asked the Commission to "extend its work in order to study," in close cooperation with the Council of Europe, the "feasibility" of establishing a European Monitoring Centre on Racism and Xenophobia (EUMC).[10] This is particularly surprising considering that newly elected president Jacques Chirac presided over the conclave only a month after Le Pen received 15 percent of the vote in the first round of the French election.

In October 1995, the council adopted two resolutions concerning racism and xenophobia, both of which expressed ambiguous support for the Kahn Commission's recommendations and clearly advocated an intergovernmental policy response. The first of these acknowledged the problem of employment discrimination but emphasized that policy action should occur within the framework of the respective powers of the EU and member states. The resolution urged member states to achieve a set of common objectives that included "guaranteeing protection for persons against all forms of discrimination on grounds of race, color, religion or national or ethnic origin" and "fighting all forms of labor discrimination against workers legally resident in each member state."[11] The second resolution focused on the role of education in combating racist and xenophobic attitudes.[12] At the June 1996 meeting in Florence, the council approved, in principle, the creation of the European Monitoring Centre on Racism and Xenophobia (EUMC).[13]

The Kahn Commission created an opportunity for influence that was exploited by both supranational institutions and transnational activists. It created a new opportunity for the SLG to engage in information politics and lobby on behalf of supranational policy action. The Kahn Commission organized national roundtable discussions in member states with government authorities as well as NGOs,[14] and the SLG participated in several of these meetings (Chopin 1999a: 3–4). In December 1994 (two months after the Kahn Commission began meeting regularly), the group devised its own proposal for a treaty amendment that it called the "Starting Point" (Chopin 1999b).

In addition, weeks after the Kahn Commission was established, the European Commission issued its *White Paper on European Social Policy* in which it suggested that "serious consideration" be given to introducing "a specific reference to combating discrimination on grounds of race, religion, age, and disability" at the "next opportunity to revise the Treaties" (European Commission 1994: 52).[15] It argued that this was necessary to realize free movement within the single market. Although the Commission resisted calls that it should use its right of legislative initiative to propose legislation, it adopted a Communication on Racism, Xenophobia, and Anti-Semitism and proposal for a Council Decision designating 1997 as the European Year Against Racism.[16] Its 1995 communication discussed the problems of racism and discrimination and finally called for the inclusion of a "general non-discrimination clause" in the treaty.[17]

The Kahn Commission altered the political context in important ways. By having an intergovernmental body recommend a treaty amendment (Bell 2002: 70), it became nearly impossible for member states not to reconsider their positions on a treaty amendment, especially in light of the European Commission's new public position and the SLG's lobbying campaign. By not amending the treaty, member states would look like they were not interested in taking action at the IGC, particularly in light of a rising radical Right. Member states realized that they could not refrain from taking some action on discrimination.

The 1996–1997 Intergovernmental Conference

The TEU that had been signed at Maastricht in 1992 provided for the treaty to be revised four years later. Accordingly, an IGC was convened in Turin on March 29, 1996, which, under the successive presidencies of Italy, Ireland, and the Netherlands, oversaw the drafting of a new treaty. The Treaty of Amsterdam was adopted by the European Council in June 1997 and signed by member states four months later. The IGC presented a unique opportunity for supranational action on antidiscrimination policy. The Kahn Commission's reports, the SLG's activities, and the European Commission's activities had all contributed to a "crescendo of voices" in support of an amendment to the treaty (Bell 2001: 82). Further, the European Commission and EP also encouraged NGOs to participate in the IGC and particularly to submit proposals concerning racism and antidiscrimination (Hix and Niessen 1997: 14). As a result, racial discrimination, which had "failed to be a central issue before 1996" (Hix and Niessen 1997: 10), was clearly on the IGC agenda.

The SLG coordinated lobbying efforts on behalf of the Starting Line proposal in the year before the IGC opened. To this end, it cooperated with local NGOs to organize a series of information seminars in the capitals of most member states (Laflache 1998: 5). These seminars were intended to generate greater awareness of the IGC and the opportunity that it offered. From these national seminars, there emerged an informal network that exchanged information concerning policy developments in the field of antidiscrimination, with particular emphasis on the positions that national governments could be expected to take at the IGC (Chopin and Niessen 1998). At the SLG's request, Simon Hix of the

London School of Economics monitored the IGC negotiations. From the start, member states, with the exception of Britain, had agreed in principle to a treaty amendment that would assign the EU competency over racial antidiscrimination policy (Hix and Niessen 1997: 59). As a result of the May 1997 British election, New Labour replaced the Euro-skeptical Conservatives at the negotiating table.

The process of drafting an actual treaty amendment raised several highly contentious and consequential issues. Based upon the ways in which these were resolved, any such amendment risked turning into yet another symbolic measure that produced no discernible policy change. Indeed, this was the outcome preferred by most member states. Here we show that member states were able to use their privileged position in the IGC negotiations to tailor a weak treaty amendment, over the objections of the SLG and the EP.[18]

The first issue concerned the nature of the treaty amendment. Specifically, would it consist merely of a general statement that condemned racism, xenophobia, and discrimination, or would it actually accord the EU competency to take policy action? And, if the latter, what would be the ambit of this new authority? In other words, would it be limited to areas in which the EU already possessed authority to act, or would it constitute a new grant of authority that extended beyond the existing parameters of the EU's power? Although most member states supported a general treaty clause that would condemn racism and prohibit racial discrimination, they were reluctant to add a specific clause that would expand the EU's competence in this area (Chopin 1999a: 1; Wallace 2000: 140). By contrast, the SLG wanted to add a new article that would expressly assign the EU competency to legislate against discrimination. Ultimately, the choice of language used in Article 13 provided an uncertain outcome.[19] Its section 1 provides:

> Without prejudice to the other provisions of this Treaty and *within the limits of the powers conferred by it upon the Community,* the Council, acting unanimously on a proposal from the Commission and after consulting the European Parliament, may take appropriate action to combat discrimination based on sex, racial or ethnic origin, religion or belief, disability, age or sexual orientation. (Article 13, TEU; emphasis added)

Rather than definitively resolving the issue one way or the other, however, the italicized language actually had the effect of confusing the matter further and rendering Article 13's meaning terribly ambiguous (Bell 2001: 82, 87–95).

As an illustration of the complex legal issues involved, law professor Mark Bell (2000: 87–95) devotes nine pages to identifying the various arguments that support an expansive versus a restrictive interpretation of the scope of authority conferred by Article 13. These arguments draw upon inferences from the article's language, the treaty's structure, European Court of Justice (ECJ) precedents, and the wording employed in non-English versions of the treaty. Bell ultimately concludes that a more limited conception of Article 13's scope is supported; thus, it "may be relied upon to prohibit discrimination *within those areas for which the Community already has competence*" (Bell 2000: 95). According to his interpretation, then, new legislation based on Article 13 would have to show that its area of application is already within the EU's competency. This would be easier to demonstrate with regard to antidiscrimination policy that targeted employment and education but not with regard to housing. The foregoing discussion illustrates the critical role of legal experts in the antidiscrimination policy area, and it highlights the potential for confusion and conflicting understandings of the final amendment's language.

The second main issue concerned whether the new treaty language would require the adoption of European antidiscrimination policy or merely create discretion for the EU to act. Ultimately, Article 13 did not require that the council take action pursuant to this new authority. This was an important element for the member states because without further action, Article 13 was merely another symbolic gesture. The third issue concerned the decisionmaking process through which any subsequent antidiscrimination policy would be formulated. According to the SLG's proposal, EU legislation would have been adopted by qualified majority voting (Chopin 1999a: 3), but here, too, member states weakened the amendment. Article 13 provides that the council can only take action with unanimous consent, thus creating the possibility that a single obstructionist state could thwart policy action. Although "the general trend in the Treaty was to extend to the Parliament the right of co-decision on legislation," the procedure for which the SLG advocated, Article 13 nevertheless consigns the EP to a purely consultative role in the legislative process.[20] This was a surprising outcome given the Parliament's prominent role in the area of antiracism and antidiscrimination (Bell 2001: 85).

Fourth, would the new treaty article exert "direct effect"?[21] When an article possess direct effect, individuals are able to invoke it in national legal proceedings and ultimately to appeal to the ECJ, which had proven to be an ally (Cichowski 2007). Thus, the SLG's proposed article would have conferred an immediate benefit upon victims of discrimination throughout the EU. In other words, would the new treaty article generate a right to nondiscrimination that could be invoked in the national legal proceedings in the absence of national implementing legislation? The Kahn Commission, the SLG, and the EP had wanted direct effect (Chopin 1999a: 3; Bell 2001: 84–85).

Finally, on what grounds would discrimination be prohibited? Because it was concerned with the plight of third-country nationals, the SLG wanted nationality included as a ground upon which discrimination could be prohibited. The Kahn Commission, too, had recommended that the amendment's protection against discrimination should apply irrespective of an individual's citizenship status (Kahn Commission 1995: 59). The commission, like the Starting Point, recommended application on the grounds of nationality and religion. Ultimately, Article 13 transferred competency to the EU in the area of discrimination on grounds of sex, racial or ethnic origin, religion or belief, disability, age, or sexual orientation.

The Racial Equality Directive

In October 1999, the month before the European Commission released its proposals for implementing Article 13, radical Right parties stunned Europe by making dramatic gains at the polls in Austria and Switzerland. At Austria's October 3, 1999, parliamentary election, the FPÖ, led by anti-immigrant politician Jörg Haider, won the second largest number of votes. After protracted negotiations, it formed a coalition government with the Austrian People's Party in February 2000. Three weeks after Austrians went to the polls, Swiss voters reinforced perceptions of a rising radical Right in Europe. Campaigning against the country's asylum policy and efforts to join the EU, the Swiss People's Party won 23 percent of the vote, up from 15 percent at the previous election, making it the second largest bloc in the lower house of Parliament and undermining a long-standing power-sharing arrangement. Although Switzerland was not a member of the EU, these developments stoked fears among European political elites.

The EU responded to the FPÖ's electoral performance with unprecedented action, including a bilateral diplomatic boycott. At the time, the council was composed of largely left-leaning governments, and all three of Europe's major powers were controlled by social democratic governments. In 1997, Tony Blair's New Labour had defeated Britain's Conservatives, and the Socialist Party won control of the French National Assembly; the following year, the government of German chancellor Helmut Kohl was replaced by a coalition of the Social Democrats (SPD) and Greens. Fourteen of the EU's foreign ministers threatened to isolate Austria if it let the FPÖ into government. Some national governments took especially prominent public positions against Austria. For example, Belgian foreign minister, Louis Michel, called for a boycott of Austrian skiing holidays (Black 2000). The French and Belgian ministers made a point of leaving the room when Austria's social affairs minister, Elisabeth Sickl, a member of the FPÖ, started to address an EU meeting (Staunton 2000). In March 2000, a month after the coalition government was formed, Haider stepped down as the FPÖ's party leader, although he retained his position as governor of the province of Carinthia.

Discussions on the Racial Equality Directive (RED) began on February 13, 2000, the very month that the FPÖ entered into a coalition government. The timing of these events created a perfect opportunity for the members of the European Commission and the SLG to shame member states into action on the proposed directive. On February 4, the *Deutsche Presse-Agentur* quoted a spokesperson for EU social affairs commissioner Anna Diamantopoulou: "it is very important that given the current situation in Austria that the EU does not delay adoption of the directives on non-discrimination on grounds of race." On February 24, 2000, Diamantopoulou called upon member states to adopt the directives in response to the events in Austria. In the words of one unnamed EU official, according to the *Deutsche Presse-Agentur*, "adoption of the proposals 'are a test for how far we are prepared to go to turn our principles into reality.'" On March 13, 2000, in the midst of the negotiations, Diamantopoulou again invoked the message that adoption of the directives would send to Haider. "To weaken these proposals," she warned, "would send entirely the wrong message at this sensitive time" (*Deutsche Presse-Agentur*).

According to Niessen (2000a: 212), the SLG believed that the Austrian situation created a favorable environment for the RED's adoption in two ways. First, it expected that Austria's new government "would not dare oppose the Race Directive out of fear that this would legitimize the reproach by the governments of the other fourteen member states that the Austrian government cannot be trusted because it includes a racist party." Second, if the other governments sought to oppose the directive, "they would be blamed and shamed for not putting their political powers where their mouth is." The SLG considered this opportunity to be short-lived. Again, according to Niessen (2000a: 212), the blaming and shaming strategy could be employed only so long as the fourteen member states maintained their pressure on Austria, a situation that the SLG estimated would "probably not last longer than one year." In addition, although it did not participate directly in the directive's negotiations, the SLG did have indirect avenues of influence that it could exploit. Key network figures maintained close contact with the commission during the negotiation process. According to Patrick Yu, who served as SLG's chair from 1997 to 2001, he "worked very closely with the Commission and also gave legal advice or counter proposals to the Commission on certain issues that arose from the negotiation process of the Racial Equality Directive." Moreover, from "conversations with the negotiators it became clear which obstacles were put in the way by which member states, leading to targeted and rapid responses at the national level" (Niessen 2000a: 212).

By the time of the RED's negotiations, there was little doubt that a racial antidiscrimination directive would be adopted, but questions remained about its policy content. In contrast to the negotiations concerning the Treaty of Amsterdam, in which member states had various options for weakening Article 13, in negotiating the RED, they had fewer options. One important negotiating point involved determining precisely where in the directive to locate particular policy commitments. Directives typically consist of preliminary "recitals" that do not have independent legal value and do not create legitimate expectations (Klimas and Vaiciukaite 2008), followed by "articles" that contain the legal commitments. Recitals must be included in all EU legislation that does not require unanimity for its adoption; thus, they were *not* required in the RED, which did require unanimous support.

The processes through which the RED was adopted illustrate the importance of cooperation between state (here EU) and societal actors. Early on, European institutions played an important role in disseminating information and analyses of a potential directive (Bell 1998). The SLG gained a great deal of what it was hoping for from its early drafts of an antidiscrimination directive. However, member states shaped the terms of the RED in ways that would preserve their sovereignty or in ways that conformed to their existing domestic policies and political forces. There is some evidence of member states amending the commission's proposal in ways that rendered the text more ambiguous, thereby providing them with greater discretion in terms of the RED's transposition. Generally speaking, council negotiations are largely insulated from partisan politics and public scrutiny, a feature that provides national governments with greater flexibility and latitude.

Conclusion

The EP first placed the issue of racism on the European agenda, and between 1984 and 1997, it consistently called for EU legislative initiatives pursuant to existing treaty authority as well as a treaty amendment that would more clearly authorize such EU action. The commission initiated European policy on racism in 1988, but member states balked and adopted a symbolic intergovernmental measure two years later. Perhaps learning from this experience, the commission refrained from expressing public support for a treaty amendment until 1994, after the council had established the Kahn Commission. Moreover, it resisted calls by NGOs to use its right of legislative initiative to propose antidiscrimination legislation and thereby place the issue on the council's agenda in the absence of a treaty amendment. The commission thus showed reluctance to get too far ahead of member state preferences. But events related to violence against ethnic minorities and the rise of the radical Right clearly had an impact on pushing forward legislation, despite hesitation on the part of member states.

The passage of the EU's Racial Equality Directive was the culmination of over fifteen years of effort to put the issues of race and racism on the European agenda. Although the European Parliament and Commission can still do more to improve representation within their own bodies, it is clear that this issue will remain on the agenda going forward. Antidiscrimination policy is an important step in the development of political opportunities for ethnic minority communities. Individuals will need to have access to opportunities in education and business in order to develop the type of credentials they will need to be attractive to political parties as potential candidates. The EU clearly has a role to play in providing incentives for countries to create a level playing field for ethnic minorities, both in the economic arena and the political arena.

Notes

1. As of 2007, of the European Parliament's 785 MEPs—representing 492 million people from 27 countries—13 are from ethnic minority backgrounds if those from Turkish/Kurdish backgrounds are included, and 5 of those are from the UK. Patrick Barkham, "Minority Report," *The Guardian,* February 13, 2007, http://www.guardian.co.uk/uk/2007/feb/14/race.eu, accessed June 14, 2011.

2. The British National Party (BNP) and the United Kingdom Independence Party (UKIP) both contested the 1999 election, with UKIP winning seven seats with an anti-immigrant and anti-EU platform.

3. Article 235 provides: "If action by the Community should prove necessary to attain, in the course of the operation of the common market, one of the objectives of the Community and this Treaty has not provided the necessary powers, the Council shall, acting unanimously on a proposal from the Commission and after consulting the Assembly, take the appropriate measures." Following the Paris Summit of October 1972, recourse to this article enabled the community to develop actions in the field of environmental, regional, social, and industrial policy.

4. Joint Declaration by the European Parliament, the European Council, and the European Commission Against Racism and Xenophobia, June 11, 1986, OJ C 158, 25.6.1986.

5. In 1997, the European Commission published a single volume that reprints the text of key EU documents concerning racism. Throughout the rest of this book, we refer to this source rather than to the original documents themselves.

6. Resolution of the European Council on the Fight Against Racism and Xenophobia, May 29, 1990 (OJ C 157, 27.6.1990).

7. This argument rests upon Article 308 (formerly Article 235). However, Article 308 did not explicitly empower the EU to act with regard to racial discrimination, but rather it authorized the EU to take actions not explicitly authorized in the treaty if such action is proven "necessary to attain, in the course of the operation of the common market, one of the objectives of the Community."

8. European Parliament, Resolution on Racism and Xenophobia, December 2, 1993; European Parliament, Resolution on Racism, Xenophobia, and Anti-Semitism, October 27, 1994; European Parliament, Resolution on Racism, Xenophobia, and Anti-Semitism, April 27, 1995; European Parliament, Resolution on Racism, Xenophobia, and Anti-Semitism, October 26, 1996; European Parliament, Report of the Committee of Civil Liberties and Internal Affairs on the Communication of the Commission on Racism, Xenophobia, and Anti-Semitism and on the Proposal for a Council Decision Designating 1997 as European Year Against Racism, April 26, 1996.

9. The German Criminal Code contains the offence of Incitement to Racial Hatred or Violence ("Volksverhetzung," § 130 Strafgesetzbuch–StGB, enacted in 1960), an offense substantially revised in 1985 and in 1994.

10. Presidency Conclusions of the European Council, Cannes, June 26–27, 1995 (para. 5), accessed at www.consilium.europa.eu/ueDocs/cms_Data /docs/pressData/en/ec/00211-C.EN5.htm on January 30, 2009.

11. Resolution of the Council on the Fight Against Racism and Xenophobia in the Fields of Employment and Social Affairs, October 5, 1995 (OJ C 296, p. 13, 10.11.1995).

12. Resolution on the Response of Educational Systems to the Problems of Racism and Xenophobia (OJ 1995 C 312/1).

13. Presidency Conclusions of the European Council, Florence, June 21–22, 1996, last accessed at www.consilium.europa.eu/ueDocs/cms_Data/docs /pressData/en/ec/032a0002.htm on January 30, 2009.

14. European Council Consultative Commission on Racism and Xenophobia, *Final Report*, Ref. 6906/1/95 Rev 1 Limite RAXEN 24 (General Secretariat of the Council of the European Union, 1995), p. 3.

15. European Commission, *European Social Policy—A Way Forward for the Union* COM (94) 333 final, 27.7.94.

16. European Commission, Communication on Racism, Xenophobia, and Anti-Semitism. Commission Communication COM (95) 653 final; European Commission, Proposal for a Council Decision Designating 1997 as the European Year Against Racism, Brussels, December 13, 1995, COM (95) 653. The proposal was adopted by the Council of Ministers 23/07/1996 C237.

17. European Commission, "Communication on Racism, Xenophobia and Anti-Semitism," COM (95) 653 final, 13.12.95, p. 18.

18. National governments and NGOs alike advanced a flurry of specific proposals (see Wallace 2000: 113–119), but we limit our focus to two sets of proposals. We examine those that were advanced by the presidency because they capture member states' positions more generally and because they ultimately shaped the outcome in important ways. And, we examine the SLG's proposal because it represents a more ambitious amendment and because many of the groups that advanced additional proposals were also part of the SLG.

19. For a more detailed analysis of the legal issues, see Griller et al. 2000: 31; Guild 2001: 65; Bell 2001: 85.

20. "European Union Anti-Discrimination Policy: From Equal Opportunities Between Women and Men to Combating Racism," Directorate-General for Research Working Document Public Liberties Series, LIBE 102 EN (Chapter 1), accessed at www.europarl.europa.eu/workingpapers/libe/102/text1_en .htm#N_13_.

21. The ECJ endorsed the position that it does not exert direct effect in *Grant v. South-West Trains* [1998] IRLR 206, para. 48.

8

Prospects for Political Integration

Martin A. Schain

At the beginning of the second decade of the twenty-first century, it is now thirty-five years or more since most countries in Western Europe decided to suspend or minimize immigration from nonwhite-sending countries. Although immigration continued—mostly, but not entirely, family unification—these populations are often thought of and referred to as "immigrants" or "descended from immigrants." As all of the chapters in this volume make clear in various ways, however, the political problem in Europe today is not immigration, but integration. In significant ways, generations of those descended from the great postwar surge of immigration from countries outside of Europe that have had long historical links to Europe through colonialism (Africa and South America) or trade (Turkey) are still perceived as outsiders, regardless of their citizenship status.

The Challenge of a Multiethnic Europe

The reference in Chapter 1 to "nonwhite immigrant-origin ethnic minorities," with a focus on "political participation," is one indication of this lack of integration, or perhaps its complexity. The concept of race has become relevant not only because "we" need to defend our dominant position from "them," but also because of what Michèle Lamont calls "standards of worth" or moral boundaries. Writing of France, she argues (on the basis of interviews) that French workers do not exclude from their moral community blacks or the poor (with whom they identify in terms of class), but "immigrants." In this way French republicanism

> delegitimizes one form of racism, but also strengthens another by drawing a clear distinction between those who share this universalistic culture (citizens) and those who do not (immigrants). This boundary is reinforced by traditional anti-Muslim feelings found in Christian France, by a lasting historical construction of French culture as superior, and by a caste-like relationship of the French with members of their former colonies. (Lamont 2000: 212–213)

Although I would question some of these conclusions with regard to blacks in France, since there is considerable evidence of exclusionary practices against black French citizens from the Caribbean as discussed by Geisser and Soum in Chapter 4 of this volume, this concept of moral boundaries is applicable to the racialization of immigrants throughout Europe and extends well beyond the first generation.

These boundaries imply two challenges. The first is the challenge of difference, which implies that immigrant groups are or are not like "us" in essential ways; the second is the challenge of whether there is a process of acceptance, which implies that immigrant groups can or cannot *become* like "us" over time. Identity, however, is not fixed, and one aspect of the challenge is the degree to which there is political resistance to an evolving identity within the host society. In this sense, the challenge is not just from immigrant groups, but within the host society as well.

In a brief article in 2010, Jürgen Habermas wrote of a developing public debate in Germany about the "Leitkultur" (a guiding national culture) that is reinforcing a movement towards xenophobia. Habermas wrote about Germany, but he could have written about a parallel process of emerging national identity throughout Europe. This process is characterized by what he terms "a relapse into [an] ethnic understanding of our liberal constitution" increasingly defined by religion.

> To the present day, the idea of the leitkultur depends on the misconception that the liberal state should demand more of its immigrants than learning the language of the country and accepting the principles of the Constitution. We had, and apparently still have, to overcome the view that immigrants are supposed to assimilate the "values" of the majority culture and to adopt its "customs." (Habermas 2010)

As the chapters in this volume make clear in various ways, in their policy discussions of national identity, European countries are caught in a tension between a dubious ethnic/religious identity, to which immigrants from Islamic countries cannot be accepted, and a civic identity that is at once more open and more accepting.

The political discourse around immigration and integration has increasingly focused on the unwillingness of immigrants to integrate, and their determination to maintain separate identities. In general, this has not been supported by the academic literature, but there have been some exceptions. Some notable scholars have seen some link between the challenge of immigration/integration to national identity, and a challenge to national security. Samuel P. Huntington, who had previously dismissed the cultural arguments that focused on the need for demanding programs of Americanization and had supported a less-demanding civic culture, embraced these arguments with fervor in his writings during the decade before his death (Huntington 2004).[1]

Christopher Caldwell's analysis is in this tradition, but in a comparative framework. He has written a deeply critical book about the emergence of a multi-ethnic society in Europe and the role of Islam in this "new" Europe. The problem, as Caldwell sees it, is Europe's inability to assimilate large numbers of immigrants in general, and Muslims in particular. The core question he asks is, "Can you have the same Europe with different people?" His answer: a clear "no." Perhaps more to the point, Caldwell sees the consequences of postwar immigration as destabilizing, dangerous, and fundamentally unjust to native European populations, who have a right to cultural stability (whatever that means) (Caldwell 2009).

For Caldwell, the real problem is Islam. All immigration, he notes, tends to erode and destabilize national cultures "that have shaped and comforted people for centuries, and it does so no matter who is doing the moving" (Caldwell 2009: 10). Islam, he says, is different in the way that it disrupts European cultural norms and raises deep questions of assimilability.

However, it is now clear that this is only part of the story. Strictly speaking, immigrant communities (those born abroad and noncitizens) have not grown in size in the old countries of immigration in Europe, although they have grown in size in some former countries of emigration in Europe (notably in Italy and Spain). On the other hand, over three generations, immigrant communities have become ethnic communities within the countries of Europe, their boundaries reinforced by racism and discrimination. The failure to adequately address discrimination has been noted in government reports, as well as by scholars (Fassin 2002: 395). Most recently, a French-US study of employment discrimination once again emphasized that it is clear that anti-Muslim discrimination is holding back Muslim economic success in France (Adida, Laitin, and Valfort 2010). So, on one hand, the policies of integration in Europe appear to be moving increasingly toward reinforcing (or reinventing) what Habermas has called "a relapse into this ethnic understanding of our liberal constitution"; on the other hand, the resistance to the acceptance of "nonwhite immigrant-origin ethnic minorities" has reinforced barriers to cultural integration. One aspect of this problem can be understood by examining political integration.

The Importance of Political Integration

Political representation can be understood as integration through politics: a pathway and a process through which the interests of immigrant groups are represented, as well as a means for developing and advancing the larger socioeconomic interests of these groups. As Richard Alba and Nancy Foner have noted, electoral success should be seen as "the gold standard" and the key to other forms of integration for the following reasons:

> First, election to political office is a direct measure of minority integration into the mainstream in the same sense that entry by minority individuals into high-status occupations is. It is an indication of a diminishment, however modest, in differentials in life chances that exist between majority and minority (Alba and Nee 2003).
>
> Second, occupation of elected political office by members of an immigrant minority gives the group a voice in decisions that can directly affect it. . . . [I]mmigrant and ethnic groups are concentrated spatially, located typically in specific cities and even in specific neighborhoods; and since most government decisions have ramifications that are spatially differentiated, they have varied effects on different population groups.
>
> Third, elected politicians usually play a powerful role in many of the routine decisions of government, which are often formally made by civil servants, such as the awarding of contracts. They also typically exert influence on the hiring of individuals to occupy public offices that are exempt from civil-service regulations; indeed, such offices may be regarded as part of the "patronage" that is the spoils of electoral victory and to be doled out to supporters.

> [Finally, the] legitimacy of a political system, especially a demo-
> cratic one, ultimately depends on its ability to give representation to
> different groups in the population. This would seem all the more true
> when the boundaries between groups are prominent and correlate with
> structures of inequality so that the boundaries effectively mark a soci-
> etal cleavage. (Alba and Foner 2009)

The argument advanced by Alba and Foner seems to make a lot of
sense, although it derives from the US experience, and is then applied
to Europe. Essentially, it argues that political representation can have
a multiplier effect that influences both the way that public resources are
distributed and opportunities that are created and given both to groups
and to individuals. As Laure Michon notes in Chapter 6 of this volume,
this analysis is supported by the work of Jane Mansbridge, Hanna
Pitkin, and Will Kymlicka. It is also presumed by many of the other articles that political integration of minority populations is both desirable
for the stability of the political system as a whole and beneficial for
minority populations, collectively and individually (see Chapters 2, 3,
and 5).

On the other hand, the relationship between representation and
enhanced minority benefits cannot be assumed and is far from automatic. In the case of the Netherlands, as Michon has demonstrated con-
vincingly in Chapter 6 of this volume:

> This helps explain why the successful inclusion of non-Western immi-
> grants in representative bodies has coincided with a controversial debate
> on immigration, integration, and the presence of Islam within Dutch so-
> ciety. Non-Western immigrant politicians have been unable to prevent
> increased restrictions on the conditions for entry to the Netherlands, a
> reduction of the subsidies for ethnic and religious organizations, the re-
> jection of the Dutch principle of "*emancipatie in eigen kring*" (eman-
> cipation in one's own community) when it comes to Islam, or more
> generally, the rise of a disrespectful tone in the public debate on how
> Muslims and Moroccans fit in Dutch society. In fact, non-Western im-
> migrant politicians have been fairly marginal to this debate.

Since political representation in the Netherlands has been demonstrably
far more extensive than anyplace else in Europe, it raises some interesting and troubling questions, the most important of which is, under what
circumstances does political integration work to the benefit of minority
communities? I would argue that by comparing Europe, in particular
France and Britain, with the United States, we can begin to understand
this complex problem.

Table 8.1 indicates that immigrant/ethnic representation is roughly similar for all three countries at the local/state levels, but sharply different at the national level, where the more porous US system has generally succeeded in providing better access than either Britain or France. Indeed, during the decade between 1996 and 2007, the representation levels of Latinos in the United States has increased by more than 50 percent at the national and state levels, compared with slightly more than 25 percent at the municipal level.[2] France has consistently had the worst record by far in this area at the national level, and the British somewhat better.

In both Europe and the United States, immigration issues have been politicized in the context of electoral politics, but the way that these issues have been framed has often been quite different. In the United States the predominant (though not the only) way of framing immigration issues has been to see immigrants as voters, if they are citizens, and potential voters, if they are not—in short, as a political resource. This way of understanding the immigration issue has been related to the development of relatively open immigration policies. Daniel Tichenor provides one answer to the question of how this way of framing the issue results in more open policies. He argues that through the nineteenth century, and then again more recently, the perceived electoral importance of immigrant voters created a dynamic, self-reinforcing mechanism. This dynamic broke down between the end of the nineteenth century and World War I, but reemerged after 1965 (Tichenor 2002). In the nineteenth century, these electoral dynamics were part of a set of "reproductive mechanisms" that reinforced one another in a path-dependent process. "Like earlier European groups, southern and eastern Europeans arrived in large numbers, easily acquired voting rights, were defended by powerful ethnic and business interests, and were courted by major party leaders" (Tichenor 2002: 148).

Progressive reforms of the early twentieth century generally undermined the power of political party leadership in both houses of Congress, and such reforms as "direct democracy" and reliance on experts for the formulation of public policy tended to undermine the role and power of political parties on the state and national levels. The weakening, then, of party control eroded the strongest political supports for an open immigration policy. Tichenor's analysis raises important questions for comparative analysis, questions that have implications for Europe that merit exploration.

Table 8.1 Political Integration of Immigrant Populations, 2004–2007 (in percentage)

	Population	Electorate	State/Local Representatives	National Representation 2004	National Representation 2006–2007
France ("visible minorities")	5.0	2.7	3.4 (large cities, 2001–2006) 8.4 (large cities, 2007)	0.0 (National Assembly) 0.6 (Senate)	0.5 (National Assembly) 1.3 (Senate)
United Kingdom	7.9	6.6	2.6 (local councils, 2006)	2.3 (House of Commons, 2005)	2.3 (House of Commons)
United States	12.5	7.4	3.2 (state assemblies and senates, 2005) 1.2 (local councils, 1992; about same in 2005)	5.3 (House of Representatives) 3.0 (Senate)	7.7 (House of Representatives) 5.0 (Senate)
The Netherlands	8.8		3.0		10.0
Germany (Turks)	3.1	1.0	0.4		0.8

Sources: Alba and Foner 2009; Department of Commerce, Bureau of the Census, 1992 Census of Governments XIII, Volume 1, Table 19; NALEO Education Fund 2007: 3; Keslassy 2009 : 27–30; Michon, this volume.

The politics of immigration has been a constant struggle in the United States related to two different kinds of electoral politics: expansion driven by seeing immigrants as a political resource; and restriction, driven by seeing immigrants as a danger to national identity or a challenge to economic well-being. Parallel to the politics of expansion has always been the politics of restriction and exclusion. At the same time that pro-immigration politics generated expansionary policies in the nineteenth century and since 1965, restrictionist politics attempted to both constrain these policies and change them. At the same time that restrictionists succeeded in closing the front gates in 1921, expansionists (often the same people) succeeded in keeping the back gates (to the Western Hemisphere) open. Expansionists then slowly opened the front gates through refugee admissions and the Hart-Celler Act in 1965. Since 1965, pro-immigration politics have dominated the political agenda, but restrictionists have had some success as well (Schain 2008: 254–256). Nevertheless, I would agree with Tichenor that both open policy and openness to immigrant/ethnic representation are related to seeing immigrants as a political resource.

Europe has been different. In the British case, and to a lesser extent in the French case, a similar set of conditions have not created a similar dynamic or a similar reproductive mechanism—generally quite the opposite. Party strategies, even when they are informed by electoral considerations, are not necessarily driven by them in the same way. Thus, in Britain and France electoral considerations tend to be driven more by identity issues that objectify immigrant populations than by strategies to mobilize emerging ethnic voters (Anwar 2001).

In Britain, New Commonwealth immigrants arrived in large numbers after World War II, easily acquired voting rights, and were courted by some Labour members of Parliament (MPs). At the very same time, however, the Labour Party and the Conservative Party proceeded to pass a series of laws that increasingly restricted entry to these very same immigrants. In addition, the decision of both British parties to converge and compromise on the issue of immigration in 1970, and neutralize their extremes, has generally served to minimize the influence of immigrant groups (Schain 2008).

In the French case, neither the Left nor the Right has been responsive to the potential of an immigrant vote. The sensitivity of immigrant voters from other parts of Europe before World War II, particularly in the Communist Party, has not been matched by electoral sensitivity to new ethnic voters from the countries of North Africa among parties of the Left.

The availability of this electorate has been somewhat delayed by French citizenship law (immigrants to Britain are eligible to vote with the establishment of residency), and their concentration in relatively few constituencies makes them less important than comparable voters in the United States. (See Table 8.2.) Nevertheless, increasingly, they are capable of providing marginal votes in presidential elections.

Explaining Differences

How then can we explain the sharp differences between Europe and the United States? Part of the difference of impact is probably institutional, the lack of a directly elected chief executive outside of France. Ethnic/immigrant voters have been important in the United States because the key states for presidential races since the nineteenth century have been those in which there are large immigrant and ethnic populations. Karen Schönwälder in Chapter 5 of this volume shows how the electoral system in Germany—of modified proportional representation at every level—minimizes the voting leverage of ethnic/immigrant voters. In addition, the broad distribution of ethnic voters throughout Germany further reduces any advantage of concentration (more about this below).

Political Parties

Whatever the institutional and structural context, the principal agents that control the access of ethnic/immigrant groups to the political system are political parties. In France, pressure from the National Front, since the early 1980s, has driven the politics of immigration in a way that has minimized considerations of ethnic voting. In part because the National Front has mobilized significant electoral support and has challenged the Left in constituencies historically dominated by the Left, the Socialist and the Communist parties have refrained from committing to more open policies of immigration, despite indications that their supporters in circumscriptions where there are concentrations of immigrants would favor such policies (Schain 2008: 115).

More generally, there is also the problem of party processes and controls, even when it appears to be logical to try to attract ethnic/immigrant votes. James Hampshire (Chapter 3) and Jonathan Laurence and Rahsaan Maxwell (Chapter 2) summarize the most important efforts of the British Labour Party to increase representation of minority candidates, and the limited success that they have achieved. In comparison with the British Labour Party, the French Socialist Party has been less disposed to see immigrant voters as a political resource, because decisions on candidates are made beyond the neighborhood level and are often dictated by national priorities (Garbaye 2005: 32). Moreover, in both Britain and France local recruitment has had little impact on national policy orientations. Relatively strong political parties in Britain and France have chosen to frame the immigration issue predominantly in identity terms, and have tended to emphasize restriction rather than openness in immigration policy.

Other factors contribute to the weakness of the reinforcing dynamic of electoral mobilization in Europe. The weak organization of immigrant groups in most countries has enhanced the ability of political parties to ignore their interests even at the local level. Immigrant groups are frequently organized at the national level, where, because of the distribution of ethnic-immigrant voters, they are likely to have the least influence.

In the United States, on the other hand, the tendency by national political parties to view ethnic/immigrant voters as a political resource grew after 1965. This tendency, with some lapses, has supported relatively open immigration policy through good and bad economic times since 1965. Moreover, in the United States, the electoral balance has tended to tip toward sensitivity to immigrant interests, in part because they are more difficult to ignore, and in part because of the incentives of both immigrant concentration and the first-past-the-post system.

Electoral Incentives

Although ethnic/immigrant voters in the United States have been important in key states for presidential races since the nineteenth century, the electoral incentives have been strengthened by the distribution of ethnic immigrant voters (and potential voters) in the United States, compared with Britain and France. While 35 percent of the congressional districts in the United States have immigrant populations of more than 10 percent, fewer than 20 percent of British parliamentary constituencies and 17 percent of circumscriptions in France have concentrations this high. In addition these congressional districts in the United States are distributed across a large number of states, but in Britain are concentrated mostly in London and the West Midlands. In the British case, the influence of these voters can be contained more easily in relatively small constituencies, and tend to weigh less heavily in major party decisions on immigration policy. The pattern is similar in France (see Table 8.2).

Table 8.2 Legislative Constituencies and Immigrant Population, 1998–2001

	Core Concentration Definition	Total Number of Constituencies	Percentage of Total Constituencies with 10 Percent or More Immigrants	Total Number with 10 Percent or More Immigrants
France	Paris and suburbs	555	16.8	93
United Kingdom	London and West Midlands	641	20	128
United States	New York and California	435	34.7	151

Source: INSEE Circonscriptions législatives: résultats du recensement de la population de mars 1999; Census results for England, Scotland, and Wales for 2001; Results of elections for 2001, House of Commons; Bureau of the Census, Congressional District Dataset, 1943–1998, E. Scott Adler, University of Colorado, Boulder, at http://socsci.colorado.edu/~esadler/Congressional_District_Data.html, accessed on April 6, 2010.

Party Commitments

Although it is generally assumed that constituencies with higher concentrations of ethnic/immigrant populations tend to be represented by
the Left, Table 8.3 suggests that while this is true for the United States
and Britain, it is not at all true for France. However, the "spectacular" results of the 2010 election in the UK, in which minority representation
among MPs for the Conservative Party increased from two to eleven
(compared with fifteen for Labour), challenges "color coding," the idea
that minority candidates are only appropriate for constituencies in which
there are large minority populations (see Chapter 3).

But what does this mean? If a majority of French circumscriptions
with concentrations of ethnic/immigrant voters are represented by the
Right, as are a third of similar congressional districts in the United
States, *how* are they represented? Do these representatives of the Right
in constituencies with high concentrations of ethnic/immigrant population speak for the perceived needs of immigrant populations, or do
they tend to frame the immigration issue in terms of identity, leaving
immigrant populations as objects of politics?

There is at least some evidence that even if political parties are sensitive to electoral considerations, they do not necessarily develop the
same strategies for dealing with concentrations of immigrants within
electoral constituencies. Thus, in Britain, while Labour MPs who represented constituencies with large numbers of ethnic voters in the
1970s tended to support relatively open immigration policies, Conservative MPs from similar constituencies framed the issue of immigration

**Table 8.3 Political Representation in Constituencies Where
Immigrants Are at Least 10 Percent of the Population**

	Percentage of Constituencies Represented by Right	Percentage of Constituencies Represented by Left
France	54	43
United Kingdom	11	89
United States	36	64

Source: INSEE Circonscriptions législatives: résultats du recensement de la population de
mars 1999 [1999 Census results for legislative districts]; Census results for England, Scotland,
and Wales for 2001; Results of elections for 2001, House of Commons; Bureau of the Census,
Congressional District Dataset, 1943–1998, E. Scott Adler, University of Colorado, Boulder, at
http://socsci.colorado.edu/~esadler/Congressional_District_Data.html, accessed on April 6,
2010.

in terms of national identity and supported highly restrictive policies (Schain 2008: 175). This supports the general assumption that parties of the Left have been more responsive to immigrant concerns than parties of the Right, even when electoral conditions are similar. Therefore, when scholars generally find some deviation from this assumption (essentially on the Left), they feel that there is something that needs to be explained (see, for example, Chapter 5).

Representation and Policy

Beyond representation, perhaps the most important difference between the United States and Europe is that in the United States there is evidence of a link between ethnic/immigrant political representation and more favorable policies, while in Europe there is not. The Dutch case, in particular, is a cautionary tale, since even where ethnic/immigrant representation is more widespread than in other European countries, ethnic influence remains constrained and limited. Hampshire argues that Labour support for antidiscrimination policies was linked to an attempt by Labour to be more responsive to minority concerns. While this appears to have been true, it seems to have been defined in terms of representation, rather than policy. Policy responsiveness, in this sense, was greatest before 1987, when there were no minority MPs from either of the major parties, and less important after 1987, when minority representation grew from four to fifteen MPs for Labour.

Several of the chapters in this volume provide evidence for an increase in representation, or at least efforts in that direction. Schönwälder (Chapter 5) and Laurence and Maxwell (Chapter 2) note that the promotion of immigrant representation has increased among parties of the German Left during the past decade, and that more recently all of the major parties have actively targeted immigrant voters. Laurence and Maxwell document the considerable commitment of the major parties on the Right and the Left in France to recruit minorities ("diversity candidates"), as well as the modest results they have achieved. In 2007, seventeen black deputies were elected to the National Assembly, sixteen of whom are from French overseas territories, and none of whom are of immigrant extraction. Nevertheless these chapters indicate that minority mobilization within political parties (Britain and Germany), outside of parties (France), and in the grassroots candidate selection process (Britain) has had a small but noticeable impact on candidacies and representation at the local level.

However, the relationship between minority representation and public policy is not evident. Laurence and Maxwell focus on the report issued by Yazid Sabeg, appointed by Nicolas Sarkozy as Diversity and Equal Opportunities Commissioner in 2008. The report, if implemented, would create the most far-reaching program to promote affirmative action (Sabeg has written positively about this) and diversity in French history. However, since the report was released, the government has not acted on its recommendations. To the contrary, it forcefully promoted a broad "debate" on French national identity (with a decidedly anti-diversity tone), as well as legislation that banned the burqa in most public places and a high-profile campaign to dismantle and expel Roma communities. In Germany, the broader representation efforts have been pursued at the same time that there has been a movement of German integration policies toward narrow conceptions of national identity, which can also be found in recent Dutch policies (see Chapter 6).

The gap between representation and policy perhaps can be better understood if we consider that almost all of the policy initiatives that have benefited immigrants and minorities have had little to do with attracting the votes of this population in an electoral context. Antidiscrimination measures were initiated in Britain as a negotiated settlement between the Labour and Conservative parties as part of the agreement that was developed for immigration restriction in the 1960s. As Terri Givens and Rhonda Evans Case make clear in Chapter 7, antidiscrimination structures in most of the rest of Europe were related to the Racial Equality Directive at the European Union level. Most of the other benefits cited in these chapters are strictly representational in nature, without any link to policy, and most appear to have been initiated by the parties or governments themselves, without pressure from immigrant associations, and not in the context of any larger strategic plan.

Conclusion

It appears the "self-reinforcing electoral mechanism," so important in US politics, has never taken hold in Europe. This certainly does not mean that ethnic-immigrant interests have always won in policy conflicts in the United States (obviously not), but they have weighed in the policy debate in ways that they have not in Europe, primarily because the electoral mechanism in Europe seems to have focused almost entirely on representation rather than policy. The separation of policy initiatives beneficial to ethnic-immigrant communities from the electoral process, however, needs to be explained and analyzed more deeply.

Does this mean that political integration, meager as it is, is closer to co-optation, an enhancement of the life-chances of minority elites, rather than the "voice in decisions" for minority populations noted by Alba and Foner? Does this mean that in Europe the defense and the expression of interests of minority communities is less dependent on "their" representatives (regardless of how numerous they are), than on party elites and European agencies?

Finally, this analysis suggests three levels of ethnic-immigrant political integration. The first is symbolic representation (see Chapter 4), in which ethnic-immigrant representatives are chosen to demonstrate the "openness" of a political party, without any implication that the chosen candidate would represent any community. The second is representation linked to an ethnic-immigrant community, either chosen by a political party to attract votes, or imposed through mobilization of the community. Finally, there is representation with an understanding of benefits: either individual benefits (patron-client) or distributive benefits for the community as a whole. The chapters in this volume indicate that the first two models can be found to varying degrees in Europe, while the third is far more typical of the United States. In the near term, it would seem that these differences will persist, and only the future will tell if increased representation will lead to increased benefits for ethnic/immigrant communities in Europe.

Notes

1. See Huntington's previous position in his textbook, first published in 1981, *American Politics: The Promise of Disharmony* (Cambridge, MA: Belknap Press, 1981).

2. Department of Commerce, Bureau of the Census, *1992 Census of Governments XIII*, Volume 1, Table 19; NALEO Education Fund 2007: 3.

Acronyms

A-SPD	Arabische Sozialdemokraten (Arab Social Democrats)
BME	black and minority ethnic
BNP	British National Party
CCME	Churches' Committee for Migrants in Europe
CDA	Christian Democratic Party (Netherlands)
CDU	Christlich Demokratische Union (Christian Democratic Union)
ChU	Small Christian Party (Netherlands)
CSU	Christlich-Soziale Union (Christian Social Union) (Bavaria)
D66	Social Liberal Party (Netherlands)
DTF	Deutsch-Türkischen Forum (German Turkish Forum)
DVU	German People's Union
EP	European Parliament
EU	European Union
EUMC	European Monitoring Centre on Racism and Xenophobia
FDP	Freie Demokratische Partei (Free Democratic Party) (Germany)
FN	Front National
FPÖ	Freedom Party (Austria)
GL	Green Left Party (Netherlands)
IGC	Intergovernmental Conference
LPBS	Labour Party Black Sections
MPG	Migration Policy Group

MPs	members of Parliament
MSI	Movimento Sociale Italiano (Italian Social Movement)
NPD	Nationaldemokratische Partei (National Democratic Party) (Germany)
OSCE	Organization for Security and Cooperation in Europe
PS	Socialist Party (France)
PvdA	Partij van de Arbeid (Labour Party) (Netherlands)
RED	Racial Equality Directive
SLG	Starting Line Group
SP	Socialist Party (Netherlands)
SPD	Sozialdemokratische Partei Deutschlands (Social Democratic Party of Germany)
TCNs	third country nationals
TEEC	Treaty Establishing the European Community
TEU	Treat of European Union
UKIP	United Kingdom Independence Party
UMP	Union pour un Mouvement Populaire (Union for a Popular Movement)
VVD	Volkspartij voor Vrijheid en Democratie (Netherlands)

Bibliography

Achin, Catherine, and Sandrine Lévêque. 2006. *Femmes en politique* [Women in politics]. Paris: La Découverte, Repères collection.

Adida, Claire, David Laitin, and Marie-Anne Valfort. 2010. "Les Français musulmans sont-ils discriminés dans leur propre pays? Une étude expérimentale sur le marché du travail" [Are French Muslims discriminated against? An experimental labor market study]. French-American Foundation and Sciences Po, April.

Alba, Richard, and Nancy Foner. 2009. "Entering the Precincts of Power: Do National Differences Matter for Immigrant Minority Political Representation?" In Jennifer L. Hochschild and John H. Mollenkopf, eds., *Bringing Outsiders In: Transatlantic Perspectives on Immigrant Political Incorporation*. Cambridge, MA: Cornell University Press, pp. 277–293.

Alba, Richard, and Victor Nee. 2003. *Remaking the American Mainstream: Assimilation and Contemporary Immigration*. Cambridge: Harvard University Press.

Amiraux, Valérie, and Patrick Simon. 2006. "There Are No Minorities Here: Cultures of Scholarship and Public Debate on Immigrants and Integration in France." *International Journal of Comparative Sociology* 47(3–4): 191–215.

Anwar, Muhammad. 1986. *Race and Politics: Ethnic Minorities and the British Political System*. London: Tavistock Publications.

———. 1994. *Race and Elections: The Participation of Ethnic Minorities in Politics*. Coventry, UK: Centre for Research in Ethnic Relations, University of Warwick.

———. 2001. "The Participation of Ethnic Minorities in British Politics." *Journal of Ethnic and Migration Studies* 27(3): 533–549.

Bancel, Nicolas, Pascal Blanchard, and Françoise Vergès. 2003. *La Réplique coloniale. Essai sur une utopie* [The colonial reply: An essay on utopia]. Paris: Albin Michel, Idées collection.

Banducci, Susan, Todd Donovan, and Jeffrey Karp. 2004. "Minority Representation, Empowerment, and Participation." *Journal of Politics* 66(2): 534–556.

Barlow, M. 2000. "Amsterdam and the Question of Metropolitan Government." In L. Deben, W. Heinemeijer, and D. van der Vaar, eds., *Understanding Amsterdam, Essays on Economic Vitality, City Life and Urban Form.* Amsterdam: Het Spinhuis, pp. 249–299.

Barreto, Matt, Gary Segura, and Nathan Woods. 2004. "The Mobilizing Effect of Majority-Minority Districts on Latino Turnout." *American Political Science Review* 98(1): 65–75.

Bell, Mark. 1998. *EU Antidiscrimination Policy: From Equal Opportunities Between Women and Men to Combating Racism.* Brussels: European Parliament Directorate General for Research.

———. 2000. "The New Article 13 EC Treaty: A Platform for a European Policy Against Racism." In Gay Moon, ed., *Race Discrimination: Developing and Using a New Legal Framework.* Portland, OR: Hart Publishing, pp. 81–112.

———. 2001. "Meeting the Challenge? A Comparison Between the EU Racial Equality Directive and the Starting Line." In Isabelle Chopin and Jan Niessen, eds., *The Starting Line and the Incorporation of the Racial Equality Directive into the National Laws of the EU Member States and Accession States.* London/Brussels: Commission for Racial Equality/Migration Policy Group, pp. 22–54.

———. 2002. *Anti-Discrimination Law and the European Union.* Oxford: Oxford University Press.

Bertelsmann Stiftung. 2008. Deutscher Städtetag and Deutscher Städte- u. Gemeindebund, eds. "Beruf Bürgermeister/in: Eine Bestandsaufnahme für Deutschland" [Mayor's occupations: An inventory for Germany]. Available from www.bertelsmann-stiftung.de/bst/de/media/xcms_bst_dms _23926_23927_2.pdf.

Bertossi, Christophe, and Jan Willem Duyendak, ed. 2009. Dossier: "Modèles d'intégration et intégration des modèles" [Models of integration and integration of models]. *Migrations Société* 21 (122) (March–April): 25–281.

Bevelander, Pieter, and Ravi Pendakur. 2008. "Electoral Participation of Natives, Immigrants, and Descendants in Sweden." Paper presented at the IMISCOE B3 Workshop on Substate, Suprastate, and National Citizenship, Edinburgh, May 15–16, 2008.

Bird, Karen. 2003. "The Political Representation of Women and Ethnic Minorities in Established Democracies: A Framework for Comparative Research." Working Paper presented for the Academy of Migration Studies in Denmark (AMID), Aalborg University, November 11.

————. 2005. "The Political Representation of Visible Minorities in Electoral Democracies: A Comparison of France, Denmark, and Canada." *Nationalism and Ethnic Politics* 11(4): 425–465.

Bird, Karen, Thomas Saalfield, and Andreas Wüst, eds. 2010. *The Political Representation of Immigrants and Minorities: Voters, Parties and Parliaments in Liberal Democracies.* London: Routledge.

Birnbaum, Pierre, ed. 1990. *Histoire politique des juifs de France: Entre universalisme et particularisme* [A political history of French Jews: Between universalism and particularism]. Paris: Presses de Sciences Po.

Black, Ian. 2000. "Austrian Leader Asks for a Chance." *The Guardian* (London), March 9, p. 16.

Bleich, Eric, and Mary Clare Feldmann. 2004. "The Rise of Race? Europeanization and Antiracist Policymaking in the EU." Paper presented at the conference *The Impact of Europeanization on Politics and Policy in Europe: Trends and Trajectories,* Toronto, University of Toronto, May 7–9.

Blerald, Philippe-Alain. 1991. "Théorie du marché politique et rationalité des politiques publiques" [A theory of the political market and the rationality of public policy]. *Revue Française de Science Politique* 41(2): 235–263.

Bömermann, Hartmut, Klaus Rehkämper, and Ulrike Rockmann. 2008. "Neue Daten zur Bevölkerung mit Migrationshintergrund in Berlin zum Stand 31.12.2007" [New data on population with immigration background] *Zeitschrift für amtliche Statistik* [Newsletter for official statistics) *Berlin Brandenburg,* no. 3 (2008): 20–28.

Borella, François. 1990. *Les Partis politiques dans la France d'aujourd'hui* [Contemporary French political parties]. Paris: Éditions de Seuil.

Bösch, Frank. 2001. "Die politische Integration der Flüchtlinge und Vertriebenen und ihre Einbindung in die CDU" [The political integration of refugees and displaced persons and their integration into the CDU]. In Rainer Schulze, ed., *Zwischen Heimat und Zuhause. Deutsche Flüchtlinge und Vertriebene in (West-) Deutschland 1945–2000* [Between homeland and home: German refugees and displaced persons in (West) Germany, 1945–2000]. Osnabrück: Secolo, pp. 107–125.

Bourdieu, Pierre. 2000. *Propos sur le champ politique* [Thoughts on the field of politics]. Lyon: Presses Universitaires de Lyon.

Brouard, Sylvain, and Vincent Tiberj. 2011. *As French As Everyone Else? A Survey of French Citizens of Maghrebin, African, and Turkish Origin.* Philadelphia, PA: Temple University Press.

Brubaker, Rogers. 1992. *Citizenship and Nationhood in France and Germany.* Cambridge: Harvard University Press.

Caldwell, Christopher. 2009. *Reflections on the Revolution in Europe: Immigration, Islam and the West.* New York: Doubleday.

Calvès, Gwénaële. 2008. *La discrimination positive* [Positive discrimination]. Paris: Presses Universitaires de France.

Castles, Stephen, and Mark Miller. 2009. *The Age of Migration: International Population Movements in the Modern World,* 4th ed. London: Macmillan, and New York: Guilford Books.

CDU. 2010. "Bundesvorstand der CDU Deutschlands, Berliner Erklärung Unsere Perspektiven 2010–2013" [National Executive of the CDU, Our perspectives on the Berlin Declaration]. Decision from January 14 and 15, 2010, Berlin, www.cdu.de.

Centraal Bureau voor de Statistiek. 2010. www.cbs.nl (accessed February 21, 2010).

Chalmers, Damian. 2000. "The Mistakes of the Good European?" *Queen's Papers on Europeanisation,* No. 7/2000.

Childs, Sarah, Joni Lovenduski, and Rosie Campbell. 2005. *Women at the Top 2005: Changing Numbers, Changing Politics?* London: Hansard Society.

Chopin, Isabelle. 1999a. *Campaigning Against Racism and Xenophobia: From a Legislative Perspective at European Level.* European Network Against Racism, Brussels (ENAR), 2.

———. 1999b. "The Starting Line Group: A Harmonised Approach to Fight Racism and to Promote Equal Treatment." *European Journal of Migration and Law* 1: 111–129.

Chopin, Isabelle, and Jan Niessen, eds. 1998. *Proposals for Legislative Measures to Combat Racism and to Promote Equal Rights in the European Union.* London: Commission for Racial Equality and the Starting Line Group.

———. 2001. *The Starting Line and the Incorporation of the Racial Equality Directive into the National Law of EU Member States and Accession States.* Brussels: Commission for Racial Equality and Migration Policy Group.

Cichowski, Rachel A. 2007. *The European Court and Civil Society: Litigation, Mobilization and Governance.* Cambridge, UK: Cambridge University Press.

Clark, Tom, Robert Putnam, and Edward Fieldhouse. 2010. *The Age of Obama: The Changing Place of Minorities in British and American Society.* Manchester: Manchester University Press.

Colas, Dominique. 2004. "La nation ethnique et républicaine de Charles De Gaulle." In *Citoyenneté et nationalité.* Paris: Gallimard Folio Histoire.

Conradt, David P. 2005. *The German Polity,* 8th ed. New York: Pearson Longman.

Cutts, David, Edward Fieldhouse, Kingsley Purdam, David Steel, and Mark Tranmer. 2007. "Voter Turnout in British South Asian Communities at the 2001 General Election." *British Journal of Politics and International Relations* 9: 396–412.

Dalton, Russell. 1988. *Citizen Politics in Western Democracies: Public Opinion and Political Parties in the United States, Great Britain, West Germany and France.* Chatham, NJ: Chatham House Publishers.

Dekker, Lisette. 2010. *Dossier: Allochtonen in de politiek* [Dossier: Ethnic minorities in politics]. Amsterdam: Instituut voor Publiek en Politiek.

Dekker, Lisette, and Brahim Fattah. 2006. "Meer diversiteit in de gemeenteraden." *IPP Nieuwsbrief Zomer 2006,* pp. 7–10.

Dienst Onderzoek en Statistiek. 2008. *Amsterdam in cijfers 2008* [Amsterdam in numbers, 2008]. Amsterdam: Dienst Onderzoek en Statistiek [Department of Research and Statistics].

Doyle, Leonard. 1993. "Unemployment and Immigration in EC Fuel Right-Wing Extremism." *The Irish Times,* September 17, p. 17.

Dummett, Ann. 1991. "Racial Equality and '1992.'" *Feminist Review* 39: 85–90.

———. 1994. "The Starting Line: A Proposal for a Draft Council Directive Concerning the Elimination of Racial Discrimination." *New Community* 20: 530–538.

Durkheim, Emile. 1964 [1895]. *The Rules of Sociological Method.* Edited by George E. G. Catlin, translated by Sarah A. Solovay and John H. Mueller. New York: The Free Press of Glenco.

Duyvendak, Jan Willem, Trees Pels, and Rally Rijkschroeff. 2009. "A Multicultural Paradise? The Cultural Factor in Dutch Integration Policy." In Jennifer Hochschild and John Mollenkopf, eds., *Bringing Outsiders In: A Transatlantic Perpsective on Immigrant Political Integration.* Ithaca, NY: Cornell University Press, pp. 129–139.

Equy, Laure, and Bastien Inzaurralde. 2007. "Candidats de la diversité: mission impossible" [Diverse candidates: Mission impossible]. *Libération,* June 4.

European Commission. 1994. *European Social Policy—A Way Forward for the Union.* COM (94) 333 final, 27.7.94.

———. 1997. *The European Institutions in the Fight Against Racism: Selected Texts.* Luxembourg: Office for the Official Publications of the European Communities.

———. 2009. "Discrimination in the EU in 2009." *Special Eurobarometer* 317.

Evrigenis Committee. 1985. "Report of the Committee of Inquiry into the Rise of Fascism and Racism in Europe" (Evrigenis Report). European Parliament.

Fanon, Frantz. 2002. *Les damnés de la terre* [The wretched of the earth]. Paris: La Découverte (original edition, 1961).

Fassin, Eric. 2002. "L'invention française de la discrimination" [The French invention of discrimination]. *Revue Française de Science Politique* 52(4): 395–415.

FAZ. 2009. "Bewerberin mit türkischen Wurzeln" [Candidate of Turkish origin]. *Frankfurter Allgemeine Zeitung,* January 23.

Federal Election Commissioner (Bundeswahlleiter). 2009. "5,6 Millionen Wahlberechtigte mit Migrationshintergrund" [5.6 million voters with an immigrant background]. Press Release, September 11.

Fennema, Meindert, and Jean Tillie. 1999. "Political Participation and Political Trust in Amsterdam: Civic Communities and Ethnic Networks." *Journal of Ethnic and Migration Studies* 25(4): 703–726.

Foner, Nancy. 2005. *In a New Land.* New York: NYU Press.

Ford, Glyn, ed. 1992. *Fascist Europe: The Rise of Racism and Xenophobia.* London: Pluto Press.

Forum. 2009. *Een divers mandaat, Hoe beleven allochtone raadsleden hun functie? 2006–2009* [A diverse mandate, do ethnic minority council members enjoy their jobs?]. Utrecht: Forum.

Fournier, Catherine. 2008. "Municipales: les chiffres qui contestent la diversité" [Municipal elections: Results that contradict diversity]. *20 Minutes*. Available at www.20minutes.fr/article/217690/Politique-Municipales-les -chiffres-qui-contestent-la-diversite.php.

Freedom House. 2005. "The Experience of the Starting Line Group Shows What Goes Up Must Come Down." Available at www.freedomhouse.hu/news /archives/issue_19_07.html.

Gabizon, Cécilia. 2008. "Les États-Unis veulent séduire les banlieues françaises" [The United States wants to seduce French suburbs]. *Le Figaro*, July 9.

Garbaye, Romain. 2005. *Getting into Local Power: The Politics of Ethnic Minorities in British and French Cities*. Malden, MA: Blackwell Publishing.

Gay, Claudine. 2001. "The Effect of Black Congressional Representation on Political Participation." *American Political Science Review* 95(3): 589– 602.

Geddes, Andrew. 1995. "The Logic of Positive Action? Ethnic Minority Representation in Britain After the 1992 General Election." *Party Politics* 1(2): 43–57.

———. 1998. "Race Related Political Participation and Representation in the UK." *Revue Européene des Migrations Internationales* 14(2): 33–50.

———. 2001. "Explaining Ethnic Minority Representation: Contemporary Trends in the Shadow of the Past." *Journal of Elections, Public Opinion, and Parties* 11(1): 119–135.

Geiger, Klaus F., and Margret Spohn. 2001. "Les parlementaires allemands issus de l'immigration" [German members of Parliament from immigrant-origin communities]. *Migrations Société* 13(77): 21–30.

Geisser, Vincent. 1997. *Ethnicité républicaine: les élites d'origine maghrébine dans le système politique français* [Republican ethnicity: Maghrebian elites in the French political system]. Paris: Presses de Sciences Po.

———. 2002. "Les femmes de l'immigration en politique: le risque de l'exotisme" [Immigrant women in politics: The risk of exoticism]. *La Lettre du FASILD* 57: 14–15.

———. 2006. "L'intégration: réflexion sur une problématique post-coloniale." In Pascal Blanchard and Nicolas Bancel, eds., *Culture post-coloniale 1961– 2006*. Paris: Autrement, Mémoire collection, pp. 145–164.

———. 2007. "Minorités visibles versus majorité invisible: promotion de la diversité ou de la diversion?" [Visible minorities versus an invisible majority: Promotion of diversity or a diversion?]. *Migrations-Société* 19 (111–112): 5–15.

Geisser, Vincent, and El Yamin Soum. 2008. *Discriminer pour mieux régner. Enquête sur la diversité dans les partis politiques.* [Discriminate to rule better: A study of diversity in political parties]. Paris: Les Éditions de l'Atelier.

Ghazli, Mourad. 2008. "Pas d'Obeurmania dans les partis" [No Obeurmania in the political parties]. *Oumma TV.* Available at www.oummatv.tv/Pas-d -Obeurmania-dans-les-partis.

Gibson, Rachel. 2002. *The Growth of Anti-Immigrant Parties in Western Europe.* Lewiston: Edwin Mellon Press.

Givens, Terri. 2005. *Voting Radical Right in Western Europe.* Cambridge: Cambridge University Press.

Gordon, Milton. 1964. *Assimilation in American Life: The Role of Race, Religion, and National Origins.* New York: Oxford University Press.

Griller, Stefan, Dimitri P. Droutsas, Gerda Falkner, Katrin Forgó, and Michael Nentwich. 2000. *The Treaty of Amsterdam: Facts, Analysis, Prospects.* New York: Springer-Verlag.

Gröhe, Hermann. 2009. "Reply to a question, 26 November." Available at www.abgeordnetenwatch.de/hermann_groehe-575-37607.html.

Guild, Elspeth. 2001. "The European Union and Article 13 of the Treaty Establishing the European Community." In Gay Moon, ed., *Race Discrimination: Developing and Using a New Legal Framework.* Portland, OR: Hart Publishing, 65–79.

Habermas, Jürgen. 2010. "Leadership and Leitkultur." *The New York Times,* October 29, p. A31.

Hall, Peter. 1993. "Policy Paradigms, Social Learning, and the State: The Case of Economic Policymaking in Britain." *Comparative Politics* 25(3): 275–296.

Hampshire, James. 2005. *Citizenship and Belonging: Immigration and the Politics of Demographic Governance in Postwar Britain.* Basingstoke, UK: Palgrave.

———. 2006. "Immigration and Race Relations Policy." In Peter Dorey, ed., *The Labour Governments, 1964–70.* London: Routledge.

———. 2009. "Race." In Colin Hay et al., eds., *The Oxford Handbook of British Politics.* Oxford: Oxford University Press.

Hansen, Randall. 2000. *Citizenship and Immigration in Post-war Britain: The Institutional Origins of a Multicultural Nation.* Oxford: Oxford University Press.

Héran, François. 2010. "Inégalités, et discriminations—Pour un usage critique et responsable de l'outil statistique" [Inequality and discrimination: For a critical and responsible use of statistical tools]. Report of the Committee for the Measurement of Diversity and the Evaluation of Discrimination. Paris: Comité pour la mesure de la diversité et l'évaluation des discriminations (COMEDD).

Hix, Simon, and Jan Niessen. 1997. *Reconsidering European Migration Policies: The 1996 IGC and the Reform of the Maastricht Treaty.* Washington/ Brussels: Migration Policy Group.

HMSO. 2008. *Equality Bill—Government Response to the Consultation*, Cm. 7454, July 2008.

House of Commons. 2010. *Speaker's Conference (on Parliamentary Representation) Final Report*, HC 239-1. London: The Stationery Office.

Huntington, Samuel P. 2004. *Who Are We? The Challenges to American's National Identity*. New York: Simon and Schuster.

Inglehart, Ronald. 1971. "The Silent Revolution in Europe: Intergenerational Change in Post-Industrial Societies." *American Political Science Review* 65(4): 991–1017.

———. 1990. *Cultural Change in Advanced Industrial Society*. Princeton, NJ: Princeton University Press.

Jacobs, Dirk. 1998. *Nieuwkomers in de politiek. Het parlementaire debat omtrent kiesrecht voor vreemdelingen in Nederland en België (1970–1997)* [Newcomers in politics: The parliamentary debate about voting rights for foreigners in the Netherlands and Belgium]. Ghent: Academia Press.

Jones-Correa, Michael. 2006. "Electoral Representation of New Actors in Suburbia," unpublished manuscript.

Joppke, Christian. 2007a. "Transformation of Immigrant Integration: Civic Integration and Antidiscrimination in the Netherlands, France, and Germany." *World Politics* 59(2): 243–273.

———. 2007b. "Beyond National Models: Civic Integration Policies for Immigrants in Western Europe." *West European Politics* 30(1): 1–22.

Kahn Commission (European Council Consultative Commission on Racism and Xenophobia). 1995. "Final Report." Ref. 6906/1/95 Rev 1 Limite RAXEN 24. Brussels: General Secretariat of the Council of the European Union.

Katwala, Sunder. 2008. "A British Obama Would Now Get a Fair Chance." *Fabian Society* (November 2).

Keck, Margaret, and Kathryn Sikkink. 1998. *Activists Beyond Borders*. Ithaca: Cornell University Press.

Keslassy, Eric. 2009. *Ouvrir la politique la diversité* [A political opening toward diversity]. Paris: Institut Montaigne (January).

Klausen, Jytte. 2005. *The Islamic Challenge*. New York: Oxford University Press.

Klimas, Tadas, and Jurate Vaiciukaite. 2008. "The Law of Recitals in European Community Legislation." *ILSA Journal of International and Comparative Law* 15. Available at http://ssrn.com/abstract=1159604.

Kymlicka, Will. 1995. *Multicultural Citizenship, A Liberal Theory of Minority Rights*. New York: Oxford University Press.

Laflache, Michelynn. 1998. "Network Objectives Achieved." *The Runnymede Bulletin* 5: 309.

Lagrange, Hugues, Jonathan Laurence, Lucile Schmid, Richard Senghor, and Catherine Wihtol de Wenden. 2009. "Mésurer les discriminations et promouvoir la diversité" [Measuring discrimination and promoting diversity]. *Esprit* (May): 61–67.

Lagroye, J., B. François, and F. Sawicki. 2002. *Sociologie politique* [Political sociology], 4th ed. Paris: Presses de Sciences Po/Dalloz.

Lamont, Michèle. 2000. *The Dignity of Working Men: Morality and the Boundaries of Race, Class, and Immigration.* Cambridge, MA: Harvard University Press.

Laurence, Jonathan. 2007. *Islam and Citizenship in Germany.* Europe Report No. 181. Brussels: International Crisis Group.

———. 2009. "Nicolas Sarkozy's Faith in the Republic." *The Toqueville Review/ La Revue Toqueville* 30(1): 1–23.

———. 2012. *The Emancipation of Europe's Muslims: The State's Role in Minority Integration.* Princeton, NJ: Princeton University Press.

Laurence, Jonathan, and Justin Vaïsse. 2006. *Integrating Islam: Political and Religious Challenges in Contemporary France.* Washington, DC: Brookings Press, 2006.

Lee, Taeku. 2008. "Race, Immigration, and the Identity-to-Politics Link." *Annual Review of Political Science* 11: 457–478.

Leighley, Jan, and Arnold Vedlitz. 1999. "Race, Ethnicity, and Political Participation: Competing Models and Contrasting Explanations." *Journal of Politics* 61(4): 1092–1114.

Le Lohé, Michel. 1998. "Ethnic Minority Participation and Representation in the British Electoral System." In Shamit Saggar, ed., *Race and British Electoral Politics.* London: UCL Press, pp. 73–94.

Lépinard, Eléonore. 2007. *L'égalité introuvable: la parité, les féministes et la République* [Unattainable equality: Parity, feminists, and the Republic]. Paris: Presses de Sciences Po.

Leveau, Rémy, and Catherine Wihtol de Wenden. 2001. *La beurgeosie. Les trois âges de la vie associative issue de l'immigration* [The bourgeoisie: Three phases of associations among immigrant-origin activists]. Paris: CNRS Editions.

Lévy, Laurent. 2005. *Le spectre du communautarisme* [The specter of communitarianism]. Paris: Éditions Amsterdam.

Libération. 2007. "Plus de jeunes, plus de femmes, toujours pas de couleur" [More young people, more women, still no people of color]. *Libération,* June 18.

Lipset, Seymour, and Stein Rokkan, eds. 1967. *Party Systems and Voter Alignments: Cross-National Perspectives.* New York: Free Press.

Lovenduski, Joni. 2005. *Feminizing Politics.* Cambridge: Polity Press.

Lozès, Patrick. 2007. *Nous les Noirs de France* [We the Blacks of France]. Paris: Editions Danger Public.

Mair, Peter. 1997. *Party System Change: Approaches and Interpretations.* New York: Oxford University Press.

Mansbridge, Jane. 1999. "Should Blacks Represent Blacks and Women Represent Women? A Contingent 'Yes.'" *Journal of Politics* 61(3): 628–657.

Maxwell, Rahsaan. 2009. "Pour en finir avec un faux débat: les statistiques ethniques" [To finish a false debate: Ethnic statistics]. *En Temps Réel Cahier,* no. 40 (September).

———. 2010. "Political Participation in France Among Non-European Origin Migrants: Segregation or Integration?" *Journal of Ethnic and Migration Studies* 36(3): 425–443.

———. 2012. *Ethnic Minority Migrants in Britain and France: Integration Trade-Offs.* New York: Cambridge University Press.

Memmi, Albert. 1985. *Portrait du colonisé. Portrait du colonisateur* [Portrait of the colonized: Portrait of the colonizer]. Paris: Gallimard, Folio actuel collection.

Messina, Anthony. 1989. *Race and Party Competition in Britain.* Oxford: Oxford University (Clarendon) Press.

———. 2007. *The Logics and Politics of Post-WWII Migration to Western Europe.* New York: Cambridge University Press.

MGFFI. 2008. "Nordrhein-Westfalen: Land der neuen Integrationschancen. 1. Integrationsbericht der Landesregierung," Düsseldorf.

Michon, Laure. 2007. "Carrières politiques locales d'immigrés à Amsterdam, 1990–2007" [Local political careers of immigrants in Amsterdam, 1990–2007]. *Migrations Société* 19(114): 115–128.

———. 2011. *Ethnic Minorities in Local Politics, Comparing Amsterdam and Paris.* Dissertation. Amsterdam: Universiteit van Amsterdam.

Michon, Laure, and Floris Vermeulen. 2010. "Immigrant Political Mobilisation in Amsterdam." Paper presented at the Workshop on Immigrant Political Incorporation in Europe organized by the Max Planck Institute for the Study of Religious and Ethnic Diversity and the University of Amsterdam, Amsterdam, June 10–11.

Modood, Tariq. 2005. *Multicultural Politics: Racism, Ethnicity, and Muslims in Britain.* Edinburgh: Edinburgh University Press.

Moore, Damian. 2002. *Ethnicité et politique de la ville en France et en Grande-Bretagne* [Ethnicity and urban policy in France and Great Britain]. Paris: L'Harmattan.

Moore, Michael Scott. 2010. "Banning Burqas in Europe." *Miller-McCune,* April 28.

Muir, Hugh. 2005. "London Delivers Bloody Nose as Galloway Wins Bitter Fight." *The Guardian,* May 6.

NALEO Education Fund. 2007. *A Profile of Latino Elected Officials in the United States, and Their Progress Since 1996.* Washington, DC: NALEO.

Ndiaye, Pap. 2005. "Pour une histoire des populations noires en France: préalables théoriques." *Le Mouvement Social,* no. 213 (October–December): 91–108.

Niessen, Jan. 1998. "New EU Policies on Immigration and Integration." Migration Policy Group (MPG). Available at http://migration.uni -konstanz.de/content/center/events/de/events/niessen.htm.

————. 2000a. "The Amsterdam Treaty and NGO Responses." *European Journal of Migration and Law* 2: 203–214.

————. 2000b. "The Starting Line and the Promotion of EU Anti-discrimination Legislation: The Role of Policy Oriented Research." *Journal of International Migration and Integration* 1(4): 493–503.

Nixon, Jaqi. 1998. "The Role of Black and Asian MPs at Westminster." In Shamit Saggar, ed., *Race and British Electoral Politics.* London: UCL Press.

Norris, Pippa. 2006. "The Impact of Electoral Reform on Women's Representation." *Acta Politica* 41(2): 197–213.

Norris, Pippa, and Joni Lovenduski. 1995. *Political Recruitment: Gender, Race and Class in the British Parliament.* Cambridge: Cambridge University Press.

OBV (Operation Black Vote). 2008. *How to Achieve Better BME Political Representation.* London: HMSO.

Olivier, Laurent. 2003. "'Ambiguïtés de la democratisation partisane en France (PS, RPR, UMP)" [Ambiguities of partisan democratization in France]. *Revue française de science politique* 53(5): 761–790.

Pedersen, Mogens. 1979. "The Dynamics of European Party Systems: Changing Patterns of Electoral Volatility." *European Journal of Political Research* 7(1): 1–26.

Pitkin, Hanna F. 1972. *The Concept of Representation.* Berkeley: University of California Press.

Portes, Alejandro, and Min Zhou. 1993. "The New Second Generation: Segmented Assimilation and Its Variants Among Post-1965 Immigrant Youth." *Annals of the American Academy of Political and Social Science* 530 (November): 74–96.

Purdham, Kingsley, Edward Fieldhouse, Andrew Russell, and Virinder Kalra. 2002. *Voter Engagement Among Black and Minority Ethnic Communities.* London: Electoral Commission.

Rath, Jan. 1985. "Immigrant Candidates in the Netherlands." *Cahiers d'Etudes sur la Mediterranée Orientale et le Monde Turco-Iranien* 1: 46–62.

Rentoul, John, et al. 1996. "Labour Blow as All-Women Lists Outlawed." *The Independent*, January 9. Available at www.independent.co.uk/news/labour -blow-as-allwomen-lists-outlawed-1323046.html.

Rinaudo, Christian. 1999. *L'ethnicité dans la cité. Jeux et enjeux de la catégorisation ethnique* [Ethnicity in urban space: The complexity of ethnic categorization]. Paris: L'Harmattan, Logiques sociales collection.

Roman, Joël. 2006. *Eux et Nous* [Them and us]. Paris: Hachette Littératures.

Ruzza, Carlo. 2000. "Anti-Racism and EU Institutions." *Journal of European Integration* 22(2): 145–171.

Sabeg, Yazid. 2009. "Programme d'action et recommandations pour la diversité et l'égalité des chances" [A program of action and recommendations for diversity and equal opportunity]. Available from www.premier-ministre .gouv.fr/IMG/pdf/Rapport_Commissariat_diversite.pdf.

Saggar, Shamit. 1997. "Racial Politics." *Parliamentary Affairs* 50: 693–707.

——. 1998a. "British South Asian Elites and Political Participation: Testing the Cultural Thesis." *Revue Européenne des Migrations Internationales* 14(2): 51–69.

——, ed. 1998b. *Race and British Electoral Politics*. London: UCL Press.

——. 2001. *Race and Political Recruitment: Ethnic Pluralism and Candidate Selection in British Political Parties*. London: Hansard Society.

Saggar, Shamit, and Andrew Geddes. 2000. "Negative and Positive Racialisation: Re-examining Ethnic Minority Political Representation in the UK." *Journal of Ethnic and Migration Studies* 26(1): 25–44.

Salin, Franck. 2007. "George Pau-Langevin: 'je voulais montrer que la diversité, c'était possible'—Entretien avec la députée socialiste de la XXe arrondissement de Paris" [George Pau Langevin: "I want to show that diversity is possible"—Interview with the Socialist Deputy from the 20th arrondissement in Paris]. *Afrik.com,* June 21.

Schaatsbergen, Reinout. 2006. "De geschiedenis van Amsterdam" [The history of Amsterdam]. Gemeente Amsterdam. Available from www.amsterdam .nl/stad_in_beeld/geschiedenis/de_geschiedenis_van (accessed January 22, 2009).

Schain, Martin A. 2008. *The Politics of Immigration in France, Britain and the United States*. New York: Palgrave/Macmillan.

Schnapper, Dominique. 1991. *La France de l'intégration. Sociologie de la nation en 1990*. Paris: Gallimard-nrf.

Schönwälder, Karen, and Christiane Kofri. 2010. "Diversity in Germany's Political Life? Immigrants in City Councils." Working Paper. Göttingen: Max Planck Institut zur Erforschung multireligiöser und multiethnischer Gesellschaften.

Schönwälder, Karen, and Janina Söhn. 2009. "Immigrant Settlement Structures in Germany: General Patterns and Urban Levels of Concentration of Major Groups." *Urban Studies* 46(7): 1439–1460.

Schulte, Addie. 2009. "Fel debat Marcouch en Baâdoud" [Fierce debate Marcouch and Baadoud]. *Het Parool* (Amsterdam), April 12.

Sewell, Terri. 1993. *Black Tribunes: Black Political Participation in Britain*. London: Lawrence Wishart.

Shamir, Michal. 1984. "Are Western Party Systems 'Frozen'? A Comparative Dynamic Analysis." *Comparative Political Studies* 17(1): 35–79.

Shukra, Kalbir. 1998a. *The Changing Pattern of Black Politics in Britain*. London: Pluto Press.

——. 1998b. "New Labour Debates and Dilemmas." In Shamit Saggar, ed., *Race and British Electoral Politics*. London: UCL Press, pp. 117–144.

Simmons, Harvey. 1996. *The French National Front: The Extremist Challenge to Democracy*. Boulder, CO: Westview Press.

Simon, Patrick. 1998. "Nationalité et origine dans la statistique française: les catégories ambiguës" [Citizenship and origins in French statistics: Ambiguous categories]. *Population* 53(3): 541–568.

———. 2007. "Comment la lutte contre les discriminations est passée à droite" [How the fight against discrimination has been taken over by the right wing]. *Mouvements*, no. 52: 153–163.

———. 2010. "Statistics, French Social Sciences and Ethnic and Racial Social Relations." *Revue française de sociologie* 51(5): 159–174.

Sineau, Mariette. 2001. *Profession femme politique. Sexe et pouvoir sous la Cinquième République* [The profession of woman politician: Sex and power in the Fifth Republic]. Paris: Presses de Sciences Po.

Small, Stephen, and John Solomos. 2006. "Race, Immigration and Politics in Britain." *International Journal of Comparative Sociology* 47(3–4): 235–257.

Smith, Ben. 2008. "Ethnic Minorities in Politics, Government and Public Life." House of Commons Library, Standard Note SN/SG/1156.

Sniderman, Paul, and Louk Hagendoorn. 2007. *When Ways of Life Collide: Multiculturalism and Its Discontents in the Netherlands*. Princeton, NJ: Princeton University Press.

Solomos, John, and Les Back. 1991. "Black Political Mobilisation and the Struggle for Equality." *Sociological Review* 39(2): 215–237.

———. 1995. *Race, Politics, and Social Change*. London: Routledge.

SPD. 2010. Arbeitsprogramm 2010 des SPD-Parteivorstandes [Party program 2010 of the SPD party leadership], January 18. Available from www .spd.de.

Stadt Dortmund. 2009. Wahlkurzbericht. Kommunalwahlen am August 30, 2009 [Short election report: Community election on August 30, 2009].

Stadt Köln. 2008. Kölner Statistische Nachrichten [Cologne statistical news] 1/2008, Statistisches Jahrbuch [Statistical yearbook] 2007, 86. Jahrgang.

———. 2009. Die Kölner Stadtteile in Zahlen, 1. Jg [The city of Cologne in numbers].

Statistisches Bundesamt [Federal Statistical Office]. 2007. Bevölkerung und Erwerbstätigkeit—Ergebnisse des Mikrozensus 2007 [Population and employment—results of the 2007 microcensus]. Fachserie 1 Reihe 2.2, Wiesbaden.

———. 2010. Presseerklärung Nr.033 [Press release 33], January 26.

Staunton, Denis. 2000. "Haider Sparks Off Fresh Controversy by Accusing Turks of Refusing to Integrate; Austria's New Government Is Snubbed at Lisbon Meeting." *The Irish Times*, February 12, p. 15.

Stöss, Richard. 1984. "Der Gesamtdeutsche Block/BHE." In Richard Stöss, ed., *Parteien-Handbuch. Die Parteien der Bundesrepublik Deutschland 1945–1980* [Party handbook: The parties of the Federal Republic of Germany, 1945–1980]. Opladen: Westdeutscher, pp. 1424–1459.

Street, Alex. 2011. "The Electoral Impact of Minority Candidates in Germany." Presented at the Annual Meeting for the American Political Science Association, September 1–4, 2011, Seattle, Washington.

Tabet, Marie-Christine. 2009. "Diversité: Encore peu d'élus" [Diversity: Still not many elected officials]. *Journal du Dimanche*, January 18.

Taraud, Christelle. 2008. *La colonization* [Colonization]. Paris: Le Cavalier Bleu, Idées reçues collection.

Thomson, Alice, and Rachel Sylvester. 2008. "Saturday Interview: Trevor Phillips. 'Brilliant as He Is, Obama Would Not Have Got into Downing Street.'" *The Times*, November 8. Available from www.timesonline.co.uk/tol/life_and_style/men/article5110226.ece.

Tichenor, Daniel. 2002. *Dividing Lines: The Politics of Immigration Control in America*. Princeton, NJ: Princeton University Press.

Tillie, Jean. 2008. *Gedeeld land, Het multiculturele ongemak van Nederland* [Divided country: The uncomfortable multiculturalism of the Netherlands]. Amsterdam: Meulenhof.

Tjalma-den Oudsten, Hester. 2006. *Afgetreden raadsleden, motieven en ervaringen*. The Hague: SGBO.

Triadafilopoulos, Triadafilos, and Karen Schönwälder. 2011. "A Bridge or Barrier to Incorporation? Germany's 1999 Citizenship Reform in Critical Perspective." *German Politics and Society*, special issue.

Trounstine, Jessica, and Melody Valdini. 2008. "The Context Matters: The Effects of Single-Member Versus At-Large Districts on City Council Diversity." *American Journal of Political Science* 52(3): 554–569.

Vaïsse, Justin. 2009. "Du bon usage d'Obama en politique française" [The good use of Obama in French politics]. *Esprit* (February).

van den Berg, Johannes. 1983. "De toegang tot het Binnenhof. De maatschappelijke herkomst van de Tweede-Kamerleden tussen 1849 en 1970" [Access to the courtyard: The social origins of members of Parliament between 1849 and 1970]. Diss., University of Leiden. Weesp: Van Holkema and Warendorf.

Villbrandt, Jasenka. 1998. "Junge Einwanderer nicht gefragt!?" [Young Immigrant isn't asked!?]. *Stachlige Argumente* 114.

Wallace, Adrienne. 2000. "The Development of an Anti-Race Discrimination Policy in the European Union." PhD dissertation, Department of Politics, New York University.

Wiedemann, Clauda. 2006. "Politische Partizipation von Migranten und Migrantinnen." In Beate Hoecker, ed., *Politische Partizipation zwischen Konvention und Protest. Eine studienorientierte Einführung*. Opladen: Budrich Verlag.

Worbs, Susanne. 2008. "Die Einbürgerung von Ausländern in Deutschland (aus der Reihe 'Integrationsreport'" [The naturalization of foreigners in Germany (from the series "Integration Report")]. Part 3. BAMF Working Paper 17, Nürnberg, 2. Aktualisierte Auflage.

Wright, Michelle. 2004. *Becoming Black: Creating Identity in the African Diaspora*. Durham, NC: Duke University Press.

Wüst, Andreas M. 2002. *Wie wählen Neubürger? Politische Einstellungen und Wahlverhalten eingebürgerter Personen in Deutschland*. Opladen: VS-Verlag.

———. 2006. "Wahlverhalten und politische Repräsentation von Migranten" [Voting behavior and political representation of immigrants]. *Der Bürger im Staat* [The citizen in the state] 56(4): 228–234. Available from www .buergerimstaat.de/4_06/integration.pdf.

Wüst, Andreas, and Dominic Heinz. 2009. "Die politische Repräsentation von Migranten in Deutschland" [Political representation of migrants in Germany]. In Markus Linden and Winfried Thaa, eds., *Die politische Repräsentation von Fremden und Armen* [Political representation of foreigners and the poor]. Baden-Baden: Nomos, pp. 201–218.

The Contributors

Rhonda Evans Case is assistant professor in the Department of Political Science at East Carolina University, where she teaches courses on comparative politics, constitutional law, and judicial politics. Her research interests include the law and politics of constitutional design, the judicialization of public policy, and the use of international law and litigation by national human rights institutions. Her articles have appeared in the *Journal of Common Market Studies,* the *Australian Journal of Political Science,* and *Congress and the Presidency*, as well as several other edited volumes.

Vincent Geisser is researcher with the National Center for Scientific Research (CNRS) in France and is also associated with the Institute for Research and the Study of the Arab and Muslim World (IREMAM) in Aix-en-Provence and the French Institute of the Middle East in Beirut, Lebanon. He is president of the Center for Information and the Study of International Migration (CIEMI) in Paris and editor of the journal *Migrations Société*. He has published numerous books, articles, chapters, and reports and is a regular participant in the French public debates on immigration and integration.

Terri E. Givens is associate professor in the Government Department at the University of Texas at Austin. Givens has received fellowships from the Ford Foundation, the German Marshall Fund, the Max-Planck Institute for the Study of Society, and various other grants and fellowships to support her research in Europe. In addition to authoring one book, *Voting Radical Right in Western Europe*, and coediting the book *Immigration Policy and Security: U.S., European, and Commonwealth Perspectives*, she has published articles in *Political Communication*, *Comparative Political Studies*, the *Journal of Common Market Studies*, the *Policy Studies Journal*, and *Comparative European Politics*.

James Hampshire is a senior lecturer in politics at Sussex, having received his BA in modern history at the University of Oxford, an MA in political philosophy at the University of York, and a DPhil in politics. He was an ESRC postdoctoral fellow in the Department of Politics and International Relations at Oxford. Hampshire's research interests lie primarily in the fields of comparative politics and political theory, with a focus on the politics of citizenship and migration. He has published numerous articles and chapters as well as two books: *Citizenship and Belonging: Immigration and the Politics of Demographic Governance in Post-war Britain* and *The Politics of Immigration: Liberal Democracy and the Transnational Movement of People*.

Jonathan Laurence is associate professor of political science at Boston College, where he teaches courses in European politics, specializing in state-religion relations. He is also Nonresident Senior Fellow at the Brookings Institution (Washington, DC), Term Member of the Council on Foreign Relations (New York City), and was previously a fellow at the Transatlantic Academy in Washington, DC. His last book *Integrating Islam* (coauthored with Justin Vaisse) received an award from the American Library Association. In addition, he has edited *The New French Council for the Muslim Faith*, coedited *Governments and Muslim Communities in the West*, and recently published the book *The Emancipation of Europe's Muslims: The State's Role in Minority Integration*.

Rahsaan Maxwell is assistant professor of political science at the University of Massachusetts, Amherst, having received his PhD from the University of California, Berkeley. His research focuses on ethnic minority migrant integration and political behavior. He has been awarded fellowships from the Ford Foundation, the French Embassy in the United States, the DAAD (German Academic Exchange Service), and the Transatlantic Academy in Washington, DC. His work has been published in the *International Migration Review*, *Political Behavior*, *West European Politics*, *Du Bois Review*, *Journal of Ethnic and Mi-*

gration Studies, Ethnic and Racial Studies, and several edited volumes. He has also recently published the book *Ethnic Minority Migrants in Britain and France: Integration Trade-Offs.*

Laure Michon is a researcher at the Department for Research and Statistics of the City of Amsterdam. She holds a PhD in social science from the University of Amsterdam. In her dissertation (*Ethnic Minorities in Local Politics,* 2011), she studied the access to politics of ethnic minority politicians in Amsterdam and in Paris, the development of their political careers over time and their discourses on representation. Previously, she conducted several projects on the political participation of immigrants for the Institute for Migration and Ethnic Studies (IMES). She has contributed to various edited volumes with chapters on the political participation of immigrants in the Netherlands and in France, the political representation of immigrants in Amsterdam and Paris and the political mobilisation of Turks in Amsterdam (see *Turkish Studies*).

Martin A. Schain is professor of politics at New York University. Schain is the founder and former director of the Center for European Studies at NYU and former chair of the European Union Studies Association. He is coeditor of the transatlantic scholarly journal *Comparative European Politics.* Among other books, he is the author of *The Politics of Immigration in France, Britain and the United States: A Comparative Study; French Communism and Local Power;* coauthor of *Politics in France;* and coeditor and author of *Comparative Federalism: The US and EU in Comparative Perspective* and *Shadows over Europe: The Development and Impact of the Extreme Right in Europe.*

Karen Schönwälder is group leader at the Max Planck Institute for the Study of Religious and Ethnic Diversity. Previously she was head of the Programme on Intercultural Conflicts and Societal Integration at the Social Science Research Center Berlin (WZB) and Privatdozentin at the Free University Berlin. Past positions include a lectureship at the University of London and a semester as visiting professor at Haifa University, Israel. Schönwälder is a member of the editorial board for *Blätter für Deutsche und Internationale Politik.* Her research interests concern political and broader societal responses to migration processes and the establishment of new minorities as well as various aspects of immigrant integration.

El Yamine Soum is a French sociologist who received his PhD from the Center for Analysis and Sociological Interventions (CADIS) in the School for Advanced Studies in the Social Sciences (École des hautes études en sciences sociales, EHESS). He has published numerous works on the topic of immigration and integration, including the book *Discriminer pour mieux régner* coauthored with Vincent Geisser.

Index

Accountability politics, 113–114

Affirmative action programs, 2, 41, 140

Afghan immigrants, 69, 82(n10)

Africadom, 31(n10)

African immigrants: Germany's immigrant electorate, 69

Akgün, Lale, 19, 67, 73

All-black and minority ethnic (BME) representation: Conservative Party's diversification strategy, 44–45; controversy over underrepresentation strategies, 33–34; diminishing need for, 8; equality rhetoric and equality guarantees, 43–48; equality strategy typology, 39–40; explaining underrepresentation, 37–40; future of shortlists, 48–51; ministerial posts, 51(n7); Parliamentary Speaker's Conference, 47–48; race relations paradigm, 41–43; UK's history of, 34–37

Allochtoon (Dutch of foreign origin), 88, 104(n3)

Alternative Liste (Germany), 75

Anti-Semitism, 58

Antidiscrimination and antiracism legislation: Article 13, 115–118;

colonial and postcolonial immigrants' citizenship rights, 51(n6); EP response to the radical Right's racism and xenophobia, 110–111; EU's authority to act, 125(n7); European Parliament's role in development of, 9, 107–108; Intergovernmental Conference, 118–121; Kahn Commission, 115; overcoming France's republican treatment of minority candidates, 53–54; Racial Equality Directive, 3, 5, 9, 122, 140; Starting Line Group, 112–115; UK's Labour governments, 51(n4); UK's race relations paradigm, 41; underrepresentation of minorities, 43–44

Arab Social Democrats, 24–25

Arslan, Bülent, 20

Article 13, 110, 115, 118–121, 123

Asian immigrants: German representation, 67; Germany's immigrant electorate, 69

Assimilation. *See* Integration and assimilation

Aubry, Martine, 18

Aussiedlers (ethnic German return-immigrants), 70, 78

165

immigrants, 97–98; UK, 51(n5)

Clegg, Nick, 45

Clubs, immigrant-origin, 24

Colonialism: allochthonous Dutch MPs, 88; Dutch of non-Western immigrant background, 104(n2); policymakers ignoring racism and discrimination, 3–4. *See also* Postcolonialism

Color coding: party commitment to minority representation, 138–139; UK's BME candidates, 37–38, 40, 49

Colorblindness: UK's race relations paradigm, 41

Commission on Racial Equality (UK), 112

Committee of Inquiry (European Parliament), 109–110

Commonwealth countries, 33, 51(n1), 134

Communist Party (France), 135

Conservative Party (Germany), 76, 78

Conservative Party (UK): "nasty party" image, 44–45; BME politics and representation, 35–36; electoral liability thesis, 38; number of ethnic minority MPs by party, UK general elections, 1979–2010, 35(table), 49; open primaries, 52(n8); party commitment to minority representation, 138–139; postwar immigration and integration, 134; priority list (A-list), 49–50

Constituencies: German two-vote system, 82(n7); legislative constituencies and immigrant populations, 1998–2001, 137(table); party commitment to minority representation, 138–139; political representation in constituencies where immigrants are at least 10 percent of the population, 138(table); role in immigrant political representation, 71

Constitution (French), 128–129

Council of Europe, 116–117

Croation immigrants, 79

Cultural racism, Islamophobia as, 6

Dagdelen, Sevim, 19, 80

Delanoë, Bertrand, 26

Demand-side barriers to BME representation, 37–40

Descriptive representation: non-Western immigrant politicians in the Netherlands, 94–95; substantive representation and, 7, 87; United Kingdom, 36–37

Deutsche Presse-Agentur newspaper, 122

Diamantapoulou, Anna, 122

Direct democracy, 132

Direct effect, 120–121, 126(n21)

Discrimination: as obstacle to political participation, 5; controversy over integration and, 2; European ethnic communities, 130; Starting Line Group combating, 112–115. *See also* Antidiscrimination and antiracism legislation; Racism

Discursive commitments to increasing diversity, 39–40

Diversity and Equal Opportunities Commission (France), 140

Diversity discourse: ethnic lobbying, 58–59; formal organization by immigrants, 21–25; France's nationalist multiculturalism, 63–64; immigrant efforts at diversification, 20–29; migrants' political legitimacy, 59; radical Right shifting policy from multiculturalism, 13–14; West European parties' diversification through recruitment, 15–17

Duncan Smith, Iain, 44

Dutch Antilles: non-Western immigrants in the Netherlands, 91(table)

East Germany, 84(n26), 109

Eastern Europe: Germany's immigrant electorate, 69–70

Economic market: French diversity discourse perpetuating discrimination, 57–58

See also France; Germany; Netherlands; United Kingdom
European Year Against Racism (1997), 117
Evrigenis Committee, 109–111, 113
Exclusion policies, 134
Exoticism, political, 56
Expansionist policies, 134
Explicit racism, 38

Fabian Society, 47, 50
Far-right parties. *See* Radical Right
Fascism, 110. *See also* Radical Right
Federal leadership: Conservatives increasing electorate through inclusion of immigrants, 78–80; Germany's ethnic representation, 67–68; Germany's residential concentration and ethnic representation, 73
Financial barriers to BME representation, 38
Ford Report, 111
France: acknowledging racial issues, 4; Article 13, 115; CDR organization for diversification, 31(n4); diversity and national identity, 63–64; elected officeholders of non-European origin, 17(table); electoral incentives for political integration, 136; equality rhetoric, 8; ethnic business in politics, 57–58; ethnic hierarchy of political roles and status, 59–62; ethnic lobbying, 58–59; ethnicity and invisibility, 60–61; Gaullist ideology, 63; gender- and ethnic-based division of labor, 57; generational politics in migrant communities, 61–62; grassroots mobilization of immigrant constituencies, 28–29; Indigenous Code, 64(n2); informal lobbying for diversification, 25; internal pressure groups, 23–24; legislative constituencies and immigrant populations, 1998–2001, 137(table); links between ethnic/immigrant representation and favorable policies, 139;

migrant communities' formal organization, 21–25; moral boundaries between citizens and immigrants, 128–129; Parity Law, 64(n5); party commitment to minority representation, 138–139; party politics controlling integration, 135–136; political career goals, 105(n16); political exoticism, 56; political integration of immigrant populations, 2004–2007, 133(table); political representation in constituencies where immigrants are at least 10 percent of the population, 138(table); political rights of colonial migrants, 53–54; postcolonial ethnic elites, 62; postcolonial gender issues, 60; pre- and post-war immigration and integration policies, 134–135; promoting visible minorities, 55; radical Right resurgence, 108, 115–116; recruiting minority candidates, 17–19; Starting Line Group, 112
France Plus, 62
Free Democratic Party (FDP; Germany), 24–25, 78–79
Freedom Party (FPÖ; Austria), 109, 121–123
Freeman, Gary, 10(n1)

Gaullist ideology, 63
Gender roles: France's division of political labor, 57; France's Parity Law, 64(n5); France's postcolonial gender issues, 60
Generational politics: Germany's immigrant electorate, 70
Genocide: Holocaust, 3–5
Geographic context of political representation, 7
German People's Union (DVU), 108–109
German-Turkish Forum, 24–25
Germany: Article 13 as response to racism, 115; development of immigrant representation, 75–78; electoral system minimizing ethnic voting leverage, 135; force of the

Women: financial barriers to
representation, 38; France's
division of political labor, 57;
France's political exoticism, 56;
gender balance across Dutch
immigrant MPs, 90; German
women's ethnic representation,
84(n29); non-Western immigrant
councilors in the Netherlands, 91;
Pau-Langevin's election, 25–26;
UK party shortlists, 34, 46–47;
UK's Conservative Party A-list,
50
World War II, 3–4

Xenophobia, 2; EP response to the
radical Right, 109–111; Germany's
Leitkultur, 128–129;
Intergovernmental Conference
on racism, 119; Kahn
Commission, 115–118; radical
Right promulgating, 109. *See
also* Antidiscrimination and
antiracism legislation;
Discrimination; Racism

Youth issues: France, 61–62
Yugoslav immigrants in Germany, 72,
84(n34)

About the Book

Do ethnic minority politicians play a meaningful role in Western Europe? How do European publics feel about nonwhite politicians? How are political parties reaching out to ethnic minority communities, and how do those communities feel about their political influence?

Addressing these increasingly critical questions, the authors of *Immigrant Politics* explore the realities, possibilities, and problems of ethnic minority and immigrant political participation in Western Europe. Their combination of thematic chapters and country studies provides a thorough overview of the politics of race and representation in the region.

Terri E. Givens is associate professor of government at the University of Texas at Austin. Her publications include *Voting Radical Right in Western Europe* and the coedited *Immigration Policy and Security*. **Rahsaan Maxwell** is assistant professor of political science at the University of Massachusetts, Amherst. He is author of *Ethnic Minority Migrants in Britain and France: Integration Trade-Offs*.